**Praise for Olivia Mellan, Sh
and *Money Harm***

"This new edition of *Money Harmony* is a M   . ᴋᴇᴀᴅ for couples who are having money conflicts. Filled with terrific observations, advice, and helpful exercises and strategies by authors Olivia Mellan and Sherry Christie, it will help you identify your money issues, learn how to communicate more effectively, appreciate your partner's strengths, and move toward developing 'money harmony' in your relationship."
– Dorian Mintzer, Ph.D., coauthor of *The Couple's Retirement Puzzle*

"*Money Harmony* is GREAT—a practical, no-nonsense, yet gentle guide to help you change your painful money habits, from two of the pioneers: Olivia Mellan and Sherry Christie."
– Ted Klontz, Ph.D., behavioral change consultant

"Olivia Mellan is a unique voice helping individuals and couples master their moneylife with humor and compassion."
– Jean Chatzky, founder of Jean Chatzky's Money School

"Olivia Mellan, whom I consider to be the godmother of financial planning, was helping clients build healthier relationships with money before the rest of us knew what financial therapy was. In this new edition of *Money Harmony*, she and Sherry Christie have made a helpful book even better. Its exercises and communication tools, especially valuable for couples, also make it a useful resource for financial planners."
– Rick Kahler, CFP®, President of Kahler Financial Group and coauthor of *Conscious Finance* and *The Financial Wisdom of Ebenezer Scrooge*

"In *Money Harmony*, Olivia Mellan gives us the work of someone who has confronted her own irrationalities and coached thousands of others to lift the money veil that prevents us from discovering our partner and others with whom we have relationships—and may have prevented us from loving ourselves as well. If the fear of looking in depth at your relationship with money makes you hesitate to read this book, then do it for the people you love."
– **Warren Farrell, Ph.D.,** author of *Why Men Earn More: The Startling Truth Behind the Pay Gap – and What Women Can Do About It*

"*Money Harmony,* in a clear and easy prose style, hits a home run for couples and individuals seeking guidance and peace about money. The latest neuroscience about gender and a Money Personality Quiz help the reader understand her relationship to money and develop compassion for her partner's or spouse's money differences."
– **Vicki Robin,** author of *Your Money or Your Life*

"I love Olivia Mellan's groundbreaking work with money personality types and gender differences. With this new edition of *Money Harmony*, everyone can benefit from her powerful tools to resolve money conflicts."
– **T. Harv Eker,** author of #1 NY Times Bestseller *Secrets of the Millionaire Mind*™

"Olivia Mellan and Sherry Christie have done it again! With the latest edition of *Money Harmony*, they offer an invaluable resource to individuals, couples, and the financial advisors who serve them."
– **Kathleen Burns Kingsbury,** author of *How to Give Financial Advice to Women* and *How to Give Financial Advice to Couples*

"While most studies include money in typical couple conflicts, *Money Harmony* is among the few that focus particularly on different

male-female dynamics around money. Citing variations in personality and brain structure, the authors have provided couples and individuals with an amazingly insightful narrative of how to bring differences into harmony. I recommend this book to all couples."
– **Harville Hendrix, Ph.D.,** co-author with Helen LaKelly Hunt of *Making Marriage Simple: Ten Truths to Change the Relationship You Have into the Relationship You Want*

"As an admirer of Olivia Mellan's money harmony work for years, I've been recommending her books to university students and others on my TV show. With this updated version, Mellan and Christie have improved an already excellent resource for both singles and couples."
– **Kelvin Boston,** best-selling author and host of PBS' "Moneywise"

"I have suggested *Money Harmony* to countless shopaholic clients. When they and their partners read about the money personalities that Olivia Mellan has identified and the way these personalities manifest in relationships, it's always an 'aha' moment. Her guidelines help each money type become better balanced by transforming that 'aha' moment into a motivating and achievable plan of action. Mellan and Christie's *Money Harmony* is unique in the field—an invaluable and practical resource."
– **April Lane Benson, Ph.D.,** author of *To Buy or Not to Buy: Why We Overshop and How to Stop* and founder of Stopping Overshopping, LLC

"Olivia Mellan and Sherry Christie's *Money Harmony: A Road Map for Individuals and Couples* will help you find your way through your personal maze of attitudes, beliefs, and feelings about money. The ideas in the book will improve your own relationship with money, and with your mate."
– **Maggie Baker, Ph.D.,** author of *Crazy About Money: How Emotions Confuse Our Money Choices and What To Do About It*

"No one settles money conflicts better than Olivia Mellan. In this new edition of *Money Harmony*, she'll help you achieve the serenity and balance you want in your moneylife."

– **Ken and Daria Dolan,** personal finance experts and former co-hosts of a nationally syndicated radio show

"Whether you know it or not, you have a relationship with money; and like any relationship, it can be healthy or not. Olivia Mellan's life-work is to guide you along the path toward a healthy, harmonious relationship with money. Read and learn."

– **James J. Green,** Editorial Director, Investment Advisor Group

MONEY HARMONY

A ROAD MAP FOR INDIVIDUALS AND COUPLES

Revised and Updated Second Edition

OLIVIA MELLAN
and SHERRY CHRISTIE

Authors of *Overcoming Overspending:*
A Winning Plan for Spenders and Their Partners

Foreword by Janet Bodnar
Editor of *Kiplinger's Personal Finance*

Illustrations by Peaches McMoon

To Michael, after all these years, still my favorite money mentor.
Olivia

To Harry, for 33 years still the one I love.
Sherry

OTHER BOOKS BY OLIVIA MELLAN & SHERRY CHRISTIE

Overcoming Overspending: A Winning Plan for Spenders and Their Partners
Money Shy to Money Sure: A Woman's Road Map to Financial Well-Being
The Client Connection: How Advisors Can Build Bridges That Last
The Advisor's Guide to Money Psychology: Taking the Fear Out of Financial Decision-Making

MONEY
HARMONY

CONTENTS

FOREWORD
BY JANET BODNAR

EDITOR OF *KIPLINGER'S PERSONAL FINANCE*

When I was working on *Raising Money Smart Kids*, my book about kids and money, I wanted to find an expert who could speak about personality traits and gender differences that help determine our attitudes toward money. I knew of Olivia Mellan's reputation as a psychotherapist who dealt with money issues, so I sought her out to get her insights. I was impressed with the way she addressed these issues without resorting to psych-speak. Her descriptions of money personalities—hoarders and spenders, "money monks" and money amassers, money worriers and money avoiders—were immediately recognizable and right on target. Not only that, her prescriptions for how to resolve conflicts in relationships where opposing personalities seemed destined to clash were grounded in common sense.

With this new edition of her classic *Money Harmony*, co-authored with Sherry Christie, Mellan shares with readers her professional expertise and her experience with thousands of patients. I guarantee that every reader will find in this book something that resonates with him or her—how your family experiences as a child helped shape your attitudes toward money as an adult, and how those attitudes, for better or worse, affect your dealings with others. For example, as

Editor of *Kiplinger's Personal Finance* magazine, I was particularly interested in chapter 6, in which Mellan and Christie tackle the issue of how men and women differ in their tolerance for risk when it comes to investing.

This is not a heavy psychological tome, but a user-friendly guide that cuts to the chase with quizzes, real-life case studies and exercises that are easy to put into practice. And Mellan offers plenty of encouragement. In the chapter on setting goals, she observes that goals which at first seem to conflict "may not be mutually exclusive after all" and shows couples how to agree on an action plan. When couples seem polarized in their attitudes, she promises to provide the "tools you need to begin restoring harmony in your relationship." And *Money Harmony* delivers.

INTRODUCTION
BY OLIVIA

Almost everyone is uncomfortable talking about money. In my psychotherapy practice, I've noticed that my clients have trouble discussing money without getting irrational and upset. In fact, it's sometimes easier for them to talk about sex or childhood trauma than about their moneylife!

Way back in the early 1980s, it was clear to me that money was the last taboo—not just in the therapist's office, but in life in general. Sadly, for a number of us that's still the case. Why? Because in our culture, money usually represents much more than dollars and cents. It's tied up with our deepest emotional needs for love, power, security, independence, control, and self-worth. And since we're usually unaware that money carries this emotional load, we fight over it without understanding what the battles are about or how to settle them.

As we grow up, few of us are provided with good examples of how to talk about money. Nor are we taught how to use it wisely. On the contrary, we're bombarded with ads urging us to buy the coolest, newest, biggest, fastest "stuff." Easily obtainable credit encourages us to gratify ourselves instantly instead of budgeting and saving for what we want. These messages have contributed to a nationwide epidemic of overspending and debt. It's not just households; many state governments and even Congress also believe in "spend now, pay later."

Along with those of us who succumb to the temptation to overspend, there are others who hoard money and/or worry about it incessantly. When a hoarder and a spender come together, disagreement is almost inevitable. One may want to save every penny, while the other would rather spend at least some of it on enjoyable purchases or experiences.

That's not the only pattern of conflict. Almost all couples tend to polarize into oppositional attitudes and behaviors about money. One may think amassing money is the key to happiness, while the other considers it debasing or corrupting. If one worries about money constantly, the other avoids dealing with money at all. If one wants to combine their money in joint accounts, the other wants to keep at least some money separate. If one loves financial risk-taking, the other is terrified of it.

You know couples like these, don't you? Maybe you're in this kind of relationship yourself. No wonder money is one of the leading causes of marital strife!

Once I became aware of these polarization patterns, I began to help my clients understand how their differences arose and find ways to resolve them, so they could share goals and make more rational financial decisions for the future.

A workbook I created for these clients was discovered by a New York publisher, who asked me to write the original *Money Harmony*. At about the same time I was interviewed by Sherry Christie, a financial writer, whose article about my couples work ended up being the best I had ever seen. When my publisher agreed to bring her on board to help me complete my next book, *Overcoming Overspending*, I was delighted. With her financial writing expertise added to my ideas and money therapy experience, it's a work marriage made in heaven. Since

1996 we have published five books together—including this revised edition of *Money Harmony*.

How Is Your Relationship with Money Going?

When helping individuals and couples to explore their relationship with money in workshops and seminars, I advise them to think of money like a person. How is the relationship going? Is it running smoothly? Or is it charged with possessive feelings, envy, anxiety, or shame? Maybe it's an arm's-length relationship, indicating that they'd rather not have anything to do with money.

Think about this for a moment. How would you describe your own relationship with money? If you have a partner, does that change the way you feel about money?

Many of us have a relationship with money that's out of balance. We need to recalibrate back to a state of equilibrium that I refer to as "money harmony."

You may be saying at this point, "My relationship with money is unbalanced only because I don't have enough of it!" But money harmony comes from within. If you are already out of balance and you come into some money, you'll just become a little more out of balance. If you're an overspender, you will overspend more wildly. If you're a compulsive saver, you will save more compulsively. An avoider will become even more reluctant to deal with money, and a worrier will worry more intensely about it. Only by achieving money harmony within yourself will you be able to find satisfaction and fulfillment, whether you have more money or less money than you do now.

In other words, money harmony isn't just a philosophy to help resolve money conflicts. It's an essential state of being for anyone who wishes to cope successfully with today's financial uncertainties.

How Sherry and I Can Help You Move
Toward Money Harmony

Most of us have a relationship with money that's clouded by anxiety, guilt, shame, secrecy, or fear. By reading the chapters of *Money Harmony*, doing the self-awareness exercises, and practicing some of the assignments, you will learn tools and insights to manage your money more rationally and confidently. If you have a partner, you'll learn to communicate with him or her more honestly and openly. And no matter whether you're in a relationship or on your own, *Money Harmony* will help you understand and improve the way you think of and act around money. Here are some examples:

- Suppose you are unexpectedly laid off after years of competent, well-respected work. You feel angry, scared, and depressed, especially if you have been brought up to shoulder the "provider burden" for your family. Arguments with your spouse escalate, and you seem to always be yelling at the kids. In *Money Harmony* you'll learn how to separate your sense of self-worth from your current misfortune, so you can handle this temporary crisis without taking out your frustrations on your family.
- Does the thought of balancing your checkbook, paying bills on time, and other money management tasks make you feel overwhelmed? The insights and exercises in *Money Harmony* will help you understand and overcome your avoidance.
- If scars from a previous experience are impairing the way you deal with money in a new relationship, you'll learn how to forge healthier attitudes and behaviors that are not dominated by past history.
- If your relationship is under stress because you earn more than your partner (an increasingly common situation, especially

when a laid-off breadwinner is forced to take a lower-paying job), *Money Harmony* can help you come to grips with this challenge and devise ways to cope with it.

PART I: YOU

Part I of *Money Harmony* is a detailed guide to exploring your personal relationship with money. In chapter 1 you'll begin by assessing the basic strengths and weaknesses of this relationship, and take our Money Personality Quiz to identify your money type or types (Spender, Hoarder, Avoider, and so on). In chapter 2 you'll look back on your own history with money, focusing on the people and events that helped shape your current attitudes and behaviors.

Chapter 3 describes—and debunks—such common myths as "Money = Love" or "Money = Power" that may be keeping you from handling your money rationally. You'll explore your money personality more fully in chapter 4, with assignments for "practicing the nonhabitual" that enable you to move away from limiting habits and attitudes. In chapter 5 you'll learn to create your own Money Dialogue, which can produce a wealth of information about where you are today and where you need to go to reach balance in your relationship with money.

PART II: YOU AND YOUR PARTNER

The second part of *Money Harmony* focuses on couples in their moneylife together, making it useful not just for romantic partners but also for parents and children, or business partners. You'll gain insight into the dynamics of your relationship and learn valuable conflict resolution skills. In chapter 6 you'll discover male-female differences that can cause relationship conflicts. In chapter 7 you'll explore a variety of couples polarization patterns such as Hoarder vs. Spender, Planner vs. Dreamer, Money Worrier vs. Money Avoider, and learn what to do if you and your partner are embroiled in a perpetual tug-of-war. Chapter 8 gives you a variety of techniques for creating a safe, positive climate of respect in which to discuss and harmonize your differences.

In chapter 9 you'll walk through a "structured moneytalk," in which you can become better acquainted with your partner's money history and learn to share your own in a way that promotes intimacy. In chapter 10 you'll learn how to conduct a structured moneytalk on some emotionally charged issue that you and your partner have had trouble resolving up to now. Finally, in chapter 11 you'll find some helpful guidelines for setting individual and joint goals.

The examples in this book, drawn from clients encountered in psychotherapy, workshops, and seminars, will help you see how other individuals and couples have struggled with and resolved difficult issues around money. To protect their privacy, their names and other details have been changed.

A Resource for Therapists and Advisors, Too

Money Harmony can be a useful guide for psychotherapists and other mental health professionals who need to help clients resolve conflicts around money. Therapists who have their own anxieties and issues with money will find that *Money Harmony* can help them feel more comfortable (perhaps for the first time) exploring financially related issues.

After reading *Money Harmony,* financial professionals will better understand why couples may lash out at each other over money matters in their office, and why other clients may freeze up or bolt out the door when presented with a perfectly sensible financial plan. They'll discover what steps can be taken to help their clients resolve the fears and other emotions that stand in the way of sound financial decision-making.

INTRODUCTION

How to Get the Most Out of *Money Harmony*

Read the chapters in order. If you are in a relationship, don't skip the first part of the book to get to the "couples" chapters faster. Unless you tackle your personal money issues first, you won't be able to fully participate in improving communications and decision-making with your partner.

Do all the suggested exercises. To get more out of this book, record your responses to the various questions and assignments. This will make it easy to track progress as you move toward better balance. An inexpensive spiral-bound notebook will do fine for recording your thoughts, feelings, and insights. Even if you don't write down your answers, taking time to think about them will make you more aware of your fears and irrationalities—and your strengths as well.

Pace yourself appropriately. Go through this book at the pace that works best for you (or you and your partner). Do you learn best by processing a little at a time? Or would you rather read cover-to-cover in one sitting so you can take in the big picture? Maybe you'd like the discipline of studying a new chapter at the same time every day or every week. There are no hard-and-fast rules; do whatever helps you learn most easily.

Less stress equals better learning. Try to make time for *Money Harmony* when you're feeling relaxed, not when you're in the middle of doing your taxes, paying bills, or having a knock-down, drag-out argument with your partner. You may still reap benefits when you're under stress, but at such times most of us revert to our oldest, most dysfunctional mode of behavior. In that state, it's hard to learn anything new—about money or anything else.

Take a breather when necessary, but come back soon! If you find yourself becoming tense or anxious as you work your way through the book, breathe deeply while giving yourself credit for tackling these sensitive issues. If you still feel distressed, take a break. But make a date with yourself (Part I) or your partner (Part II) to return to your reading at another time. Don't drop out for too long, or you'll lose valuable momentum.

Cultivate honesty and openness. Be as honest as possible with yourself and with your partner. When sharing the details of your private journey, you naturally need to respect your own limits (and your mate's), and you have the right to stop talking about something that makes you uncomfortable. Come back to it later when you're ready to try again. The more you can share with your partner, the more intimacy will result. And the more self-honesty you cultivate, the more effective your money harmony work will be.

Practice and monitor new actions and attitudes. You will be doing a variety of assignments whose objective is to sample new money behaviors and attitudes. Note your reactions to "doing what doesn't come naturally." Record your thoughts and feelings, both positive and negative. This will help you integrate the changes into your life.

Reward yourself for your changes. When you do the exercises, or take actions that are new and different for you, give yourself a treat for this new behavior. Choose a reward that doesn't reinforce any of your old patterns. For example, overspenders should not go out and spend big bucks!

Give yourself positive feedback. Take time to appreciate the courage and self-awareness it takes to grapple with the material in *Money Harmony*. Give yourself credit when you come to the end of each chapter, if not more often. This validation helps build the reserves necessary to increase your self-esteem and make positive changes in your life. If you keep making sincere efforts to expand your awareness and improve your behavior, it's impossible to praise yourself too much.

Tackle issues with patience and gentleness. Money harmony work can often be a slow and challenging process. Be patient with yourself and your irrationalities, and cultivate a nonjudgmental and forgiving attitude. If you're in a relationship, extend this patience and compassion to your partner as well. Remember that you (or the two of you) cannot realistically resolve all issues at once. Tackle the most difficult issues in short, manageable chunks.

Keep your sense of humor. Even though you may have painful memories or experiences around money, try to keep it in perspective. (As they say, it's only money.) Money harmony work doesn't have to be an agonizing process. In fact, it can be fun if you lighten up a bit and see the humor in your own foibles. For example, I've written spoof songs about money personality types to remind myself that I share irrational traits with hordes of other people.

The only universal rule I've heard about dealing wisely with money is "Save more, spend less, and don't do anything stupid," coined by financial planning innovator Dick Wagner of WorthLiving LLC. It's good advice. But if you develop a balanced relationship with money (or make good progress in that direction), I know your confidence and satisfaction in life will dramatically increase.

Working with *Money Harmony,* you'll see that money is *not* love, power, security, or any other magical key to life. It's just a tool to help you on your journey throughout life—one that you can learn to use in a way that reflects your values and integrity. Practice cultivating money harmony, and your self-confidence and self-esteem will rise in more ways than you can imagine.

PART ONE

MONEY HARMONY AND YOU

1.
GETTING STARTED:
FINDING YOUR BASELINE

Most of us have powerful feelings about money—so powerful that we find it difficult to make rational decisions and maintain harmonious relationships when we deal with it.

Some of us hoard money, while others spend it lavishly. We may attend diligently to financial tasks, or do our best to avoid them. Some people feel guilty about having too much; others feel ashamed of having too little. Some are afraid that dealing with money will corrupt or demean them. Some of us are conservative investors, others love taking risks, and still others are unwilling to invest at all. Some worry about money to a degree that affects the quality of their lives. And some feel a kind of free-floating financial anxiety without any idea where it comes from.

It's common to harbor a variety of feelings about money at any given time, or to switch from one set of feelings to another (for example, worrying or even obsessing about money today and completely ignoring it tomorrow). Someone may be thrifty for several months and then explode in a wild spending spree.

Do you know how you feel about money? How aware are you of the money attitudes and behaviors you exhibit every day? In this chapter, you'll gain an understanding of your relationship with money and your money personality. By increasing your self-awareness, you'll be taking an important first step in the journey toward greater money harmony.

Exercise 1: Assessing Your Strengths and Weaknesses

Let's begin by creating two lists. In the first list, note two or three aspects of your moneylife that give you pride or pleasure. Try to zero in on specifics. As we mentioned earlier, it's best to write down your responses in a notebook. If that's not possible, at least take some time to think about them.

Having trouble getting started? Consider these examples:
- I make enough money to live on.
- I balance my checkbook regularly.
- I'm a generous gift giver.
- I have more than $25,000 in savings.

For the second list, identify two or three aspects of your money-life that cause you discomfort or even shame. Examples on this list might include the following:
- I go on shopping binges now and then.
- I procrastinate about paying bills.
- I overdraw my checking account from time to time.
- Some months I can't pay off my credit card bill.
- I have trouble spending money on gifts for myself or loved ones.

After you've finished both lists, ask yourself which one was easier for you to come up with: the positive one or the negative one? Your answer will determine where you need to concentrate your attention at first. For example, if you found it easier to come up with your negative feelings and behaviors because these shortcomings prey on your mind, you'll experience more growth and healing by initially turning your attention to your positive qualities. On the other hand, if you tended to downplay or deny your negative traits, you'll profit most from concentrating first on those negatives. (Don't beat yourself up, though. Remember, nobody's perfect!)

At workshops Olivia has led, participants have learned for themselves the therapeutic value of changing their perspectives. A woman we'll call Mildred was a good example. When Mildred did this assessment exercise, she tended to praise herself for her generosity. She was initially uncomfortable focusing on her weaknesses, but creating a "negative" list made her confront the fact that she had run up huge credit card balances when she was experiencing marital stress. For the first time she felt confident about changing her overspending habits, which had been rooted in reactive anger.

Another example was a freelance writer in his 60s (we'll call him Aaron), who felt deeply ashamed of being a "stingy worrywart," as his wife and daughters constantly told him. Aaron's feelings about his relationship with money were intensely negative. When he created his "positive" list, he was amazed to realize that his Hoarder tendencies had enabled him to own a house and send both daughters to college on his modest income. This shed a whole new light on his money behavior, giving him enough self-confidence to confront with more gentleness the aspects of it that were *not* serving him or his family well.

People never change when they feel too bad about themselves. Only by validating themselves for their strengths do they have a springboard from which to confront their weaknesses.

Exercise 2: The Money Personality Quiz

Having assessed your strengths and weaknesses and the relative ease of doing the two lists, you know where you need to do your beginning work. Now you can move on to the Money Personality Quiz.

This isn't a statistically valid survey, just a way to help determine which money types prevail in your makeup. By taking the quiz, you'll see which of five major money personality types most closely matches your own tendencies: Hoarder, Spender, Money Monk, Avoider, or Amasser. (If you're the sixth type, a Money Worrier, you already know it. The quiz will help determine any other money personality traits you may share.) Bear in mind that each type has both good qualities and shortcomings, and that most people are in fact a combination of types.

To start the quiz, choose an answer for each of the 20 statements below. If you don't see an answer that describes exactly how you feel, choose the one that comes closest. Record your answers in your notebook.

Remember, there are no right answers. Just be as honest with yourself as you can—and have fun!

Money Personality Quiz

1. If $20,000 came to me unexpectedly, my first impulse would be to...
   a. Spend it on things I want, including gifts for others.
   b. Immediately put it somewhere safe so it won't get frittered away.
   c. Put off making any decisions until I felt less overwhelmed.
   d. Figure out ways of investing it to get the best possible return.
   e. Give most of it away to organizations that can make the world a better place.

2. Here's how I feel about my money:
   a. I make sure it never influences my life choices.
   b. I enjoy spending it on gifts and anything else that gives me pleasure.
   c. I think about it a lot and strategize how to make more of it.

    d. I hold onto it and enjoy thinking about the security it provides.

    e. I try not to think about it and hope it will take care of itself.

3. My primary financial objective is…
   a. To save enough money now so I never have to worry about my old age.
   b. Unclear to me.
   c. To have enough of it to make sure I can buy whatever I want.
   d. To have enough to satisfy my basic needs, and then give the rest away.
   e. To make as much of it as possible as quickly as possible.

4. Here's how I feel about budgeting:
   a. I take a lot of time figuring out how to have more money to spend and save.
   b. I take pride in following my budget closely.
   c. I take pride in living so simply that I've never needed a budget.
   d. Budget? Yuck! Just hearing the word makes me want to rebel.
   e. I don't have a budget and wouldn't know how to start making one. I hope my money will take care of itself.

5. Here's how I feel about spending:
   a. I hope I have enough money to take care of unexpected expenses.
   b. I enjoy spending money, as long as I can keep earning and saving more and my net worth keeps increasing.
   c. I'd rather save my money; spending it makes me nervous.
   d. I don't care where my money goes; I have more important things to think about.
   e. I love spending money, and I tend to spend more than I earn.

6. Here's how I feel about financial record keeping:
   a. I love to look at my old statements to see how much more money I have now.
   b. I'm not sure which records I should be keeping.
   c. I enjoy keeping careful records.
   d. I keep track of things on and off.
   e. I don't keep records. There are more important things in life.

7. Here's how I feel about saving:
   a. I know I ought to be saving money, but I never seem to get around to it.
   b. I really enjoy saving—the more, the better!
   c. I have trouble saving money, which bothers me sometimes.
   d. If I had enough money to save, I'd give it away instead.
   e. Saving comes naturally to me. I am regular and consistent about it.

8. Here's how I feel about borrowing:
   a. I try not to borrow money because it's easy to lose track of paying it back.
   b. It's rare for me to borrow money, because I always have enough saved for emergencies.
   c. I'm willing to borrow money to make money, but I dislike having lots of debt.
   d. I've borrowed money quite often, but I can't say I've always paid it back.
   e. I hate debt and would borrow only for absolute necessities.

9. Here's how I feel about lending money:
   a. I'm pretty generous and don't worry too much about getting it back.

   b. People tend not to ask me for money. They know I probably don't have any extra.

   c. I have no idea whether I could afford to lend anyone money.

   d. I try never to lend money, but if I do, I feel tense about it until it's repaid.

   e. I don't mind lending money at a good interest rate, if I get repaid on time.

10. Here's how I feel about credit cards:

   a. I don't like to use credit cards, and think that people who do are asking for trouble.

   b. I use credit cards a lot and tend to make the minimum payment most of the time.

   c. I don't mind running up a large balance, as long as I can pay it off quickly.

   d. I'm often surprised by how much I owe, especially when late fees are added in.

   e. I've always tended to avoid using credit. I prefer paying by debit card or cash.

11. In the event of a financial emergency...

   a. I don't know if I have enough saved, so I just hope for the best.

   b. I hope I could rely on friends or bartering services.

   c. I never have enough money left over to save for emergencies.

   d. I've put aside a sizable amount for emergencies, but I'm not sure it's enough.

   e. I've saved enough for almost any emergency, but hope I never have to spend it.

12. Here's how I feel about paying taxes:

   a. I'm always astonished to find out how much tax I owe.

b. I save regularly for taxes, and usually file my return well before it's due.

c. I hate the whole thing and try to get it done with as little fuss as possible.

d. I always have to scramble to get my return done and find cash to pay my taxes.

e. I take pride in paying less on my increased income, if I can.

13. To feel totally satisfied with my annual income, I would need...
   a. My employer to match every dollar I put into my 401(k).
   b. At least twice as much as I'm earning now.
   c. I'm sure I could use more money, but I have no idea how much.
   d. I'm fine the way I am. More money would make me feel uncomfortable.
   e. To have someone else pay my bills, so I can spend the whole paycheck!

14. Here's how I feel about investing:
   a. I always let my dividends compound to maximize my return.
   b. If I were to invest, I'd want someone else to make all the decisions for me.
   c. I invest only in safe, conservative choices like CDs.
   d. I've always wanted to try something wild that might end up making me rich.
   e. If I were to invest, I would choose only socially responsible companies.

15. When I really want to buy something that's not in my budget:
   a. What budget? Everything will work out all right.
   b. I have to think hard before giving myself permission to spend the money.

c. I'll buy it whether or not I can afford it.
d. Most of the things I want are not expensive, so I can afford to buy them (even though later on I'll probably wish I hadn't).
e. If it's important enough, I'll tweak my portfolio. Otherwise, I'll forget about it.

16. When I think about money in general, to me it represents...
    a. Security.
    b. Happiness, pleasure, and excitement.
    c. A sense of greed and possibly corruption.
    d. A source of anxiety and conflict.
    e. Power, prestige, and freedom.

17. I would apply for a bank loan under these circumstances:
    a. To go on vacation or buy something I really wanted.
    b. Only if it were a dire emergency. I hope I'll never have to borrow money.
    c. To invest in a business or some other high-yielding opportunity.
    d. To make essential repairs, pay for college, or increase my future security.
    e. I don't know.

18. I worry about money...
    a. Never. I worry about more important things, like global warming.
    b. Somewhat, but I'm doing all I can to make sure I'll have more than enough.
    c. Constantly. It's the main thing I worry about.
    d. Only when a financial crisis strikes.
    e. What, me worry? I just enjoy spending it!

19. Here's how I feel about providing for my future:
    a. I'm quite concerned, since it's been so hard for me to save.
    b. All I can do is hope the future will take care of itself.
    c. Since I'm planning to have plenty of money, the future will probably be fine.
    d. I feel reasonably confident, since I've been saving systematically for years.
    e. I think making a difference with one's life is much more important than money.

20. If I won a million dollars in the lottery, my first reaction would be to…
    a. Feel guilty, thinking about people who have nothing.
    b. Feel relieved that my future was now secure.
    c. Be totally overwhelmed. I would have no idea how to handle it.
    d. Start thinking about ways to make it grow and use it for my own enjoyment.
    e. Be wildly excited, realizing that from now on I could buy anything I wanted.

Now that you've completed the quiz, here's the key to determine which combination of money personality types you tend to be:

H = Hoarder, *S* = Spender, *M* = Money Monk, *V* = Avoider, *A* = Amasser

(If you're a Worrier, remember that the quiz results will show if there are also elements of another type in your money personality.)

Refer to the following list as you score your answers, keeping count of how many *H*s, *S*s, *M*s, *V*s, and *A*s you've chosen. Whichever abbreviation(s) turn up most frequently in your answers represent your predominant money personality type or types among the five delineated here.

1.	*a. S*	*b. H*	*c. V*	*d. A*	*e. M*
2.	*a. M*	*b. S*	*c. A*	*d. H*	*e. V*

3.	*a. H*	*b. V*	*c. S*	*d. M*	*e. A*
4.	*a. A*	*b. H*	*c. M*	*d. S*	*e. V*
5.	*a. V*	*b. A*	*c. H*	*d. M*	*e. S*
6.	*a. A*	*b. V*	*c. H*	*d. S*	*e. M*
7.	*a. V*	*b. A*	*c. S*	*d. M*	*e. H*
8.	*a. V*	*b. H*	*c. A*	*d. S*	*e. M*
9.	*a. S*	*b. M*	*c. V*	*d. H*	*e. A*
10.	*a. M*	*b. S*	*c. A*	*d. V*	*e. H*
11.	*a. V*	*b. M*	*c. S*	*d. A*	*e. H*
12.	*a. V*	*b. H*	*c. M*	*d. S*	*e. A*
13.	*a. H*	*b. A*	*c. V*	*d. M*	*e. S*
14.	*a. A*	*b. V*	*c. H*	*d. S*	*e. M*
15.	*a. V*	*b. H*	*c. S*	*d. M*	*e. A*
16.	*a. H*	*b. S*	*c. M*	*d. V*	*e. A*
17.	*a. S*	*b. M*	*c. A*	*d. H*	*e. V*
18.	*a. M*	*b. A*	*c. H*	*d. V*	*e. S*
19.	*a. S*	*b. V*	*c. A*	*d. H*	*e. M*
20.	*a. M*	*b. H*	*c. V*	*d. A*	*e. S*

Which Money Type Are You?

Hoarder. You enjoy holding on to your money and budgeting for what you need. It may be difficult for you to spend money on luxury items or immediate pleasures for yourself and your loved ones. For you, money equals security.

Spender. You probably love to use your money to buy whatever will make you happy. You may have a hard time saving, budgeting, and delaying gratification for long-term goals. Money equals happiness and pleasure for you.

Money Monk. You think money corrupts, and you try to avoid having too much of it. You would feel guilty and conflicted if a large amount of money unexpectedly came your way. To you, it's an evil influence—the Dark Side of the Force.

Avoider. You tend to avoid balancing your checkbook, setting spending priorities, and other financial tasks. You may feel anxious or incompetent about dealing with money. For you, money is a mystery you can't (or don't want to) understand.

Amasser. You like to keep large amounts of money on hand and to see your portfolio growing constantly. This preoccupation may be keeping you from fully enjoying your life and nonfinancial relationships in the moment. Money means prestige, power, and success to you—maybe even self-worth.

Worrier. You worry about money constantly, to the point that it affects your peace of mind. Money means nothing but anxiety to you.

As we mentioned earlier, there are other money types—for example, Money Mergers and Money Separatists, Planners and Dreamers, and Risk Takers and Risk Avoiders, to name a few. But an understanding of the six mentioned above is a great way to start getting to know your money personality.

Exercise 3: Assessing Your Money Personality

We'll explore each money type in greater detail in chapter 4. For now, just take a few minutes to answer the following questions:

1. Which money type (or types) are you?
2. Does your money personality cause you any difficulty in life, either on your own or in your relationship with a partner?
3. What are one or two things about your relationship with money that you might like to change in some way? (These changes don't have to be actions or behaviors; they can be feelings or attitudes as well.)

Need ideas to jump-start your response to question 3? Consider these examples.

I'd like to...

• Stop going on shopping binges.

- Start saving for retirement.
- Quit worrying about money so much.
- Avoid feeling guilty when I buy myself something.
- Stop sabotaging my attempts to make more money, so I can provide better for myself and my family.
- Be more conscious of where I spend my money.
- Not feel ashamed of making so much money.
- Quit procrastinating about paying bills and doing my taxes.
- Stop feeling bad that I don't earn more money.

After answering these simple questions and looking at the tendencies toward imbalance reflected in your money personality, you're ready to begin thinking about actions you can take or attitudes you can adopt to move toward more harmony in your moneylife.

Your First "Money Harmony" Assignment

Once a week, commit to doing one thing to increase your self-confidence and feelings of competence about dealing with your money. The more specific your action is, the better. Here are some examples of weekly assignments, but you're free to think up your own:

For Hoarders:
- I will spend $25 or so on some "frivolous" gift for myself.
- I won't look at my budget once all week.

For Spenders:
- I will put $20 into my savings account this week.
- I will refrain from buying anything unplanned this week.

For Money Monks:
- I will buy myself something I've wanted for a while.
- I will make a list of ways to use money that include giving to myself as well as giving to others.

For Avoiders:
- I will keep careful notes of where I spend my money this week.
- I will spend one hour on Wednesday (or whatever day works best for you) paying bills and balancing my checkbook.

For Amassers:
- I will check my investments no more than once this week.
- I will do two activities this week that don't involve money, such as going to a library or eating a brown-bag lunch in the park.

For Worriers (remember, we didn't include you in the quiz—but you know who you are):
- At a time when I am most worried about money, I will write down what I'm worried about and what I'll do if the worst happens.
- I will practice calming activities this week to counteract my anxious state.

If you choose one of these assignments, remember to monitor your reactions to it. For example, Money Monks should record how it feels to treat themselves to a "selfish" pleasure. Reward yourself for your new behavior, and give yourself credit for making a great start on the road to money harmony. These acts of "practicing the nonhabitual" will help you develop muscles you never had before and strengthen your self-esteem.

In chapter 2, you'll explore your history with money and find ways to lighten the emotional load of past experiences. By discovering how the past affects the present, you'll be able to improve the future.

2.
YOUR MONEY HISTORY: HEARING VOICES FROM THE PAST

In this chapter you'll gain insight into the influences that formed your money personality, beginning with your childhood. We'll ask you to jog your memory about your family members; your family's financial history, circumstances, and traditions; and other influences such as religious training, peer pressure, and societal communications. As we walk through a series of exercises, you'll get clearer on how your past exposure to money messages may be misinforming your present.

By taking stock of past influences on your moneylife, you will become more and more detached from these powerful voices. This will enable you to relate to money in a way that reflects your own values. It also means that if you are in a relationship, you won't be dragging along a ton of excess baggage when you deal with your partner. Or at least the baggage will be out in the open, so you can more easily move it aside.

Families Don't Talk Rationally About Money

In her seminars on money harmony, Olivia usually begins by observing that most of us grew up in families where money was never talked about. Not in a rational, helpful way, that is.

Before she adds that last qualifier, someone will inevitably object, "In my family, we talked about money all the time!" Pressed to elaborate on this, the protester will generally say something like "Well, my dad worried about not having enough money, and he yelled at my mom for spending too much."

That's not exactly what we mean by "talking about money." It's rare for children to have a true sense of their family's financial situation. It's equally rare for them to be taught in a patient and nonjudgmental way about the value of saving money, or helped to understand that many people in our society use it as a measure of self-worth, as a tool to exercise power and control, or as compensation for feeling deprived in other ways.

As a result, instead of shaping realistic opinions of our own, many of us adopt our parents' attitudes and behaviors around money without realizing it. Others of us react strongly against our parental models, vowing never to be like Dad the Worrier or Mom the Spender. In either case, we are not free to develop a relationship with money that reflects our own values and sense of integrity.

Kids Trying on Parents' Money Modes

Adopting or Rejecting Our Parents' Money Styles:
Olivia's Story

Olivia's own experience is a good example of children adopting their parents' money styles. She says, "My father tended to worry about money a lot—too much, in my opinion. My mother didn't work outside the home when I was growing up, and she often felt lonely

29

and depressed. Shopping became the way she tried to fill up her inner emptiness. It was her reward whenever she felt like celebrating, and buying me clothes was the way she showed me she loved me.

"Feeling guilty about her binges, she would come home with the new clothes she'd bought and hide them behind the living room chair until my dad was in a good mood. Then she'd model them for him, after which she felt free to integrate them into her wardrobe.

"I always thought this ritual was a little ridiculous. But to my amazement, when I was grown up and earning about as much money as the man I'd married, I found myself reenacting my dad's money anxiety and my mom's shopaholism. I would hide my own newly purchased clothes in the trunk of the car (my version of behind the living room chair) until my husband was in a good mood and I could get his approval—even though my purchases were in no way extravagant, and it was *my own money I was spending*! Until I started doing money awareness work with others, I was completely unaware that I was careening back and forth between my parents' money modes."

A woman who spoke to Olivia on a talk show (we'll call her Irma) exemplified a very different kind of reaction. Irma's father had lived through and been deeply affected by the Great Depression. When she was growing up, he would make her account for every penny of her allowance in a humiliating weekly ritual. Determined not to be a Hoarder and a Worrier like him, she became the opposite: an over-spender who avoided any money management responsibilities. Never again, she vowed, would she let any man control her with money. When her husband innocently asked for her check register so he could balance their joint checkbook, she accused him of trying to control her as her dad had.

It took only a few minutes of money awareness talk for Irma to see that her husband was *not* her father. With Olivia's help, she discovered a way to give her husband the information he needed without reopening her old wound.

By working with Irma and clients who had troubled relationships with money, Olivia got a handle on her own shopaholic tendencies and started to take steps toward changing them. "Once I realized how ludicrous it was for me to be aping my mother in hiding my purchases," she says, "I was able to stop doing it and to confide in my husband about my struggles around shopping." A little awareness of childhood money messages and vows can go a long way in helping us cast off old attitudes that now serve us poorly.

Childhood Vow #1

Exercise 1: Recalling Your Money Memories

How was money handled in your family when you were growing up? Record your memories in your notebook, or at least take some time thinking about them. These questions may help you get started:

- What was your father's attitude toward money, and how did he handle it? Was he satisfied with his work and how much he earned? If you remember interacting about money with him, what are your memories?
- What are your impressions of your mother's relationship with money? How did she feel about her work, either in or out of the house, in relation to money? If you remember interacting about money with her, what are your memories?
- What did your mother think about the way your father dealt with money? What did he think about her attitude toward money? Did the two of them talk about it? Did they agree or disagree? Did they fight?
- If you have siblings, did your parents treat all of you the same where money was involved? If not, how did it affect you?
- What are your siblings' attitudes toward money now? How are their attitudes similar to or different from your own? (Temperament may explain some differences here.)
- Did any other relatives (grandparents, godparents, aunts, uncles, cousins, etc.) influence the way you think about money? If so, how? How might these messages be affecting you today?

Childhood Vow #2

Exercise 2: Your Family's Financial Circumstances

Most of the time, direct and open communication about family finances just doesn't happen. What often does get communicated is free-floating anxiety and a general sense of malaise. This causes a lot of psychic harm and can lead to intense anxiety in children, whether or not there is any reason for worry.

Leonard's story is a prime example of this. Olivia happened to be talking on a radio show about the importance of revisiting childhood money traumas, once you have developed the maturity to exorcise these demons, when 56-year-old Leonard called in with his amazing tale. He said, "When I was a teenager working in my mother's restaurant, she was always talking about how we were on the brink of financial catastrophe. I worked day and night, even on weekends, to help us stay afloat. I had so much anxiety about it that I developed a stammer. Years later, in my living room, my mother started talking about the 'good old days' when we were making so much money in the restaurant business. I lost control and started screaming at her about all the time I spent worrying about our money that was not even based on a real financial threat! I've never yelled at my mother like that before or since. When I finished, I was amazed to realize that my stammer was gone. And it never came back."

Leonard's story is a therapist's dream: one catharsis, and a complete resolution of symptoms! Even if your own tale is less dramatic, you may remember living with a completely wrong impression of your family's financial status—or with no knowledge of it at all. Now is a good time to call up such memories with questions like these:

- Were you ever told specifically about your family's financial situation? If not, did you have a sense of being poor, comfortable, well off, or subject to fluctuating fortunes? How did this situation compare with that of your peers or neighbors?
- If you knew your family's situation, how did you react to it? Could this knowledge (or lack thereof) still be affecting you in some way?
- Did you ever feel guilty about or ashamed of how much or how little money you thought your family had, compared with others around you?
- Did either of your parents worry about money? If so, was it your mother, your father, or both of them? Did they express

their worries in front of you, or only behind closed doors? What effect did their worrying have on you?

- Did it ever seem that there was some sort of mysterious financial problem in your family? If so, how did you feel about it? Did you ever learn any money secrets that your parents had kept from you? If so, what was your reaction?

- Did you ever discover that you had a totally inaccurate picture of your family's economic status while you were growing up? If so, when and how did you learn the truth? How did you react? Do you think this faulty image affected your childhood and/or your adult life up to now?

Sometimes a child's ignorance about family finances causes a problem for the parent. Consider what happened to Henry, whose two teenage children were constantly asking him for money and complaining when he said he didn't make enough to give them any more. He felt under so much stress that he sought the help of a budget counselor at the Navy base where he was stationed. The counselor confirmed that Henry was handling his money sensibly, and told him a simple way to solve the problem with his children. She urged him to cash his next paycheck in one-dollar bills, call a family meeting around the kitchen table, and count out the money for every bill he had to pay in front of the kids. The next week, Henry came back to see the counselor, grinning from ear to ear. "You won't believe what happened," he said. "Both my thirteen-year-old and my fifteen-year-old actually apologized for giving me such a hard time and offered to find part-time work to help out!" This turnabout occurred only because Henry gave his children specific information about the family's financial circumstances.

Of course, what works with teenagers may have no effect on much younger children. The point is that when parents are willing to give their children a clear, objective, and age-appropriate view of the family finances, the two generations are more likely to become allies instead of adversaries.

Exercise 3: Money Memories Around Allowances

Families handle allowances in a variety of ways, some of which can have profound effects on children:

No allowance. Some children never receive an allowance, and thus never learn to deal with money until they're adults.

Unlimited money. Some get whatever they want from their parents, leading them to believe that money will always be there when they need it. When they grow up, they are shocked to learn that this isn't true.

Allowances with strings. Some are given an allowance with restrictions on how they can spend it. This makes them feel that the money is never really theirs. They tend to resent their parents' strictness, especially knowing that their friends can spend their allowances any way they want. Some who face restrictions on their spending also infer that their parents don't trust them to make good choices. In some cases, these people are still telling themselves as adults that they are not to be trusted with money.

Allowances based on good grades. Some are paid for getting As on their report card. This adds pressure they don't want, and makes them feel that the only reason to excel is to make money.

Ad hoc payments. One fellow who was paid for chores said that in later years, his wife complained that he never helped around the house. It occurred to him that he was probably waiting to be paid for his services!

Allocated allowances. Some children are educated to divide their allowance into different-colored jars: one for spending, the second for saving toward a desired purchase, the third for investing in a company the child chose, and the fourth for charitable giving. By teaching that money can be invested for the future or shared with others, not just spent, this method (our favorite allowance strategy) can help children learn to delay gratification for things they really want.

Let's take a look now at your own experience. If you were given an allowance, think about these questions:

- Was there anything you were supposed to do to earn it? Did you receive it consistently?
- How old were you when you started getting an allowance? How much did you receive? Was it more or less than your friends got?
- Was your allowance ever taken away as a punishment? If so, what for?
- Were you asked to account for how you spent the money?
- How did you feel about the way allowances were handled in your family? Did it lead you to any conclusions about what money meant?

Exercise 4: Family Traditions Around Money and Work

Ken was experiencing extreme anxiety attacks in graduate school, where he was studying art. He was not only his family's first college graduate, but also its first artist. Until starting therapy, he didn't realize that what he was feeling was a kind of "survivor guilt" because his father had had to leave college to support a family.

After several months in therapy, Ken started feeling more pride in his career choice, more confidence in listening to his own inner voice, and more energy to discuss with his family the courageous path he had chosen. Eventually he was able to ask for and get his father's blessing to pursue his dream. This longed-for support helped him joyfully embrace his career as an artist.

Although Ken was departing from family tradition, you may be continuing a tradition such as running the family business or going into teaching. Perhaps you're following in the footsteps of a particularly successful member of your family—your father, the distinguished doctor; your mother, the crackerjack businesswoman; or your big sister, the decorated Army officer. Let's take a closer look:

- Are you continuing a family tradition of career or philanthropy? Does adhering to this tradition work for you? If not, what's holding you back from making the changes you would like to make?
- Do you feel pressured to be as successful or wealthy as someone else in your family? Are you being urged to pursue a similar field, or to avoid that field in order not to compete? Are you okay with the way you feel about this family role model? If not, how would you like to feel?
- Are you departing from family traditions about work, spending, saving, or investing? How do you feel about it—proud, guilty, ashamed? Is this the way you would like to feel?

Exercise 5: Money Messages from Your Religious Training

Childhood religious training can instill powerful messages about money and its meanings. Some people are taught that "money is the root of all evil." (The Bible actually says, "Love of money is the root of all evil." It's a warning against greed, not against money per se.) This message may well leave a person reluctant to earn too much, or inherit too much, for fear it will lead to being corrupted.

Are similar lessons influencing you today? Consider these questions:

- What messages about money did you learn in Sunday school, catechism class, or other religious training? How did you react to these messages? What do you think about them today?

- Have you abandoned any of these old messages? How do you feel about that?
- Did any of these messages about money conflict with what else you learned (accidentally or on purpose) while growing up? If so, do you still feel conflicted? In what way? How could this conflict be resolved?

Exercise 6: Money Messages from Peers

Peers can have a strong influence on us, especially when we're young. In particular, we may compare our family's financial position with that of our friends and status leaders.

In thinking back, you may remember being much poorer—or richer—than the rest of the kids you knew. Maybe one of your class-mates didn't think twice about buying expensive clothes, while another wore her family's hand-me-downs. There was probably somebody who habitually borrowed money and never paid it back, and some-body else who tried to impress everyone by talking about what his parents were going to buy him.

Consider the messages your peers were sending and how you reacted:

- How did you feel about money when you were with your friends? Ashamed, proud, guilty, envious, anxious?
- Were any of them much richer or poorer than you? How did this affect your feelings about money and your behavior around it?
- Do you remember any specific incidents connected with your friends and money? What emotions do these memories evoke? How might they be affecting you now?

Exercise 7: Other Emotional Memories About Money

Our most emotional childhood memories about money may not come from anyone close to us. Sometimes events happen to us, or around us, that are so searing, we remember them well into adulthood. Olivia has one such indelible memory.

"Although I was extremely young—five or six years old—I remember this incident, and the feelings surrounding it, as if it were yesterday," she says. "While I was waiting in a barbershop with my dad, I watched a young boy, not much older than I was, ask his father for a quarter. His dad refused him coldly, and the little boy started to sob. As I witnessed this upsetting scene, the boy's anguish gripped me so strongly that I vowed never to feel as deprived as he did. I firmly believe that this vow contributed heavily to my overspending tendencies as an adult. Whether or not I had money, I acted as if I did."

Since she became aware of this (and other money vows), the horror of being deprived has progressively lost its grip on her psyche and on her spending behavior. Olivia now calls herself a "recovering overspender."

Is there something unforgettable you saw or heard as a child that influenced the way you feel about money now?

Exercise 8: Money Messages from Society

After many decades of saturation by television, movies, radio, magazines, and other mass media, our culture has become all about buying things to foster a desired self-image. From beautiful models posing with tail-finned sedans of the '50s to cool-looking young people texting on their latest-generation smartphones, we're told that our identity can be shaped by what we own.

In recent years advertising has become more individualized and even more pervasive, with subtle sales pitches targeting us through search page listings, Facebook posts, tweets, texts, and instant messages. Marketers can push ads directly to our phone, tablet, or PC, using data-gathering software that knows our interests and purchase patterns. Born into a sea of consumerism, we must struggle to learn how to swim in it. Those who don't learn can easily drown in debt.

Do you remember any promotional messages that influenced your financial habits or preferences?

Exercise 9: Preserving Positive Influences from Our Past

It's important to remember that we pick up positive attitudes and behaviors, not just negatives, from the people and events in our past. As an essential part of your self-exploration, consider how you would answer these questions:

- Who influenced you about money in a healthy way? Maybe your parents, other relatives, teachers, peers, or someone else you knew or read about?
- Did any childhood events have a positive effect (consciously or unconsciously) on your relationship with money?
- What money skills and attitudes did you adopt from these influences? As an adult, do you use these lessons as much as you'd like?

Exercise 10: Summarizing What You've Learned

Since we've covered a lot of ground in this chapter, it's a good idea to summarize what you've learned. Even if you haven't recorded any of your answers up to now, consider writing down your thoughts about these summary questions:

- What messages did you get from family, friends, and other influences that affect your relationship with money today?

- Are any other emotional memories around money influencing you today?
- Did you make any childhood vows that may still be controlling you?
- What positive messages from the past would you like to retain?
- What changes would you like to make so your life is less affected by the past?

Your Second "Money Harmony" Assignment

During the next week, make one change in the way you handle money that helps you feel more liberated from past influences. For example, if you normally act just like your Hoarder mother, you might decide to give away some gently used clothing that you seldom wear. Remember to pay attention to your feelings about this new behavior, and reward yourself in some way that makes you feel good about yourself.

Don't Be Surprised by Temporary Setbacks and Relapses

After doing all this positive self-awareness work, you may find that the patterns you're trying to overcome will temporarily intensify instead of abating. Don't be too upset by relapses; they're normal and should be greeted with patience and understanding. When we confront our demons and try to tame them, they often rear their ugly heads defiantly.

Growth and change usually occur in a process that is one step forward, one-half step back. Don't panic! Your greater self-awareness and your commitment to try on new attitudes and actions will keep you moving forward.

3.
MONEY MYTHS: LEARNING TO IDENTIFY AND DEBUNK FALSE BELIEFS

Money myths reflect the wonderful, almost magical things we believe money can do for us. Though each myth contains some kernel of truth, taking them as gospel can trigger intense emotions about money (anxiety, fear, obsession) and make it difficult to handle the simplest financial decisions and tasks.

Most Americans believe at least one money myth. Many of us believe a number of them. The most common myths are these six:

Money = Happiness
Money = Love
Money = Power
Money = Freedom
Money = Self-Worth
Money = Security

Are any of these money myths affecting you personally? If so, you need to look at how the problem myth(s) can be debunked. Only then will you be free to make decisions that enhance your life instead

43

of constraining it—and bring you into greater harmony with your money.

Myth #1: Money Equals Happiness

Money = Happiness

"Money equals happiness" is one of the most prevalent myths in our culture. It's represented in jokes that date back to the dawn of time. For example, you can probably complete these two quips:

"Being rich isn't everything, but _____!"
"I've been rich and I've been poor, and _____!"

You probably completed the first saying with "it's the main thing" or "it beats whatever's in second place." And we bet you finished the second one with "rich is better." Right?

Magazines and books tell us the inspiring stories of people who worked hard, became rich, and lived happily ever after. Such individuals as Oprah Winfrey, Sir Richard Branson, and the late Steve Jobs serve as the quintessential models of success. But can we ever know (a) whether such people are really happy or (b) if they are, what role money plays in their happiness?

Of course, being financially stressed definitely *does* affect happiness. As a song from an old '40s musical called *Allegro* puts it, "Money isn't everything, except when you are poor." But even then, money isn't the main driver of happiness and satisfaction. People who aren't aware of this fact will feel driven to accumulate more and more money, until this obsession crowds out the happiness they hoped it would create.

DO YOU BELIEVE MONEY = HAPPINESS?

You may think you don't believe in the "money equals happiness" myth, but how would you answer these five questions?

1. Do you tell yourself that the reason why you feel unhappy, unfulfilled, or discontented is that you don't make enough money?
2. When you encounter someone who is not as well off as you are, do you assume that the person can't be very happy?
3. Do you envy people who earn more or spend more extravagantly than you do, assuming that they must live a life of greater comfort and contentment?

4. Do you catch yourself thinking, *If only I made more money, I would be so much happier?*
5. If your own or your partner's income were slightly reduced, would that upset you tremendously?

If you replied "yes" to at least three of the five questions, the "money equals happiness" myth has its hooks in you.

Exercises to Debunk "Money = Happiness"

To begin challenging this belief, think of two activities that make you very happy. Jot them down in your notebook. Then record your responses to these next questions:

- How much does it cost to do these activities?
- Are they best done by yourself, or with others?

When doing this exercise in workshops, participants are often pleasantly surprised to realize that many things they enjoy doing involve someone else and cost little or nothing. (Making love is often on the list.) So maybe the truth is that for many of us, social connections = happiness. For others, walks in nature, quality time alone, or reading a good book are both enjoyable and fulfilling. If your responses are similar, it's proof that much of your happiness has little to do with money.

Here's another useful exercise:

- For two weeks, keep track of everything you spend money on.
- On a scale of 1 to 10, rate the fulfillment each expenditure brings you.

This exercise can be a real eye-opener, for it will show that you use your money in many ways that don't add one iota to your happiness.

If you still believe you'd be happier with more money, do one more thing: find examples that belie the "money equals happiness" myth. You probably won't have to ponder very long before thinking of people who are happy in their career, their relationships, or their volunteer work but don't have a lot of money.

For example, some years ago a magazine article[1] about wealth produced a number of reader responses that said in essence, "When I think back on the last 20 years, I realize that my husband [or my wife] and I were happiest when we were making less money. Our lives were simpler, we were more creative about doing things we wanted to do, we didn't work so hard, and we had more time and energy to enjoy life and each other. That seemed like true wealth to us."

On the other side of the coin, tabloid journalists revel in telling us about Hollywood celebrities, sports stars, and pop music legends who have money to burn but have been through multiple unhappy marriages and are beset by addictions—sometimes fatally. Being rich certainly didn't buy them happiness.

Here's a closer-to-home example. As a guest on a TV talk show, Olivia met Dennis, an earnest man who had just won the state lottery. He confessed that he'd felt unhappy and anxious ever since this sup-posedly wonderful event. He was besieged with business "opportuni-ties," and even a few marriage proposals from strange women. Once a trusting person, he had become suspicious of others. How could he tell whether someone was after his money or genuinely liked him as an individual?

This windfall had ended up making Dennis's life a living hell. Although he was learning to deal with the situation, he would be the last person on earth to say that money equals happiness. Many other lottery winners report that their sudden wealth has an immensely destabilizing effect on their lives, creating far more problems than it solves.

With so much financial uncertainty in the air these days, freeing yourself from this pervasive money myth can make it easier for you to roll with the punches. If you're denied a raise or forced to take a lower-paying job, you will tend to feel less deprived and depressed. Despite financial ups and downs, you'll stand a much better chance of getting real enjoyment out of life.

Here's a final assignment for anyone who just can't shake the myth that money equals happiness:

- Once a day for a week, spend time on activities (old or new) that cost little or nothing and make you happy.
- Notice and record your feelings about these activities.

This exercise will help you realize that there is much in life (or could be) that brings you happiness and hardly costs a thing.

Myth #2: Money Equals Love

Money = Love

Money doesn't equal happiness? Then maybe it equals love—or so we're told by many luxury-goods marketers. Buy your sweetheart a mega-carat diamond ring whose extravagance will show the world how much you care. Buy your newly graduated son a "wicked fast" sports car so he and all his pals will know the depth of your love for him. Buy your boyfriend the coolest cell phone, your mom and dad a time-share in Cabo San Lucas, your daughter a spring break trip to Paris.... It goes on and on. Many of us believe not only that money equals love, but that money can make up for a *lack* of love.

DO YOU BELIEVE MONEY = LOVE?

To see if you're among the many for whom money equals love, consider how you would answer these five questions:

1. When you feel lonely, depressed, or unloved, do you go out and buy something to cheer yourself up?
2. When you want to celebrate a job well done, do you immediately think of buying yourself a gift?
3. When you go into a shop, is it hard for you to leave until you've bought something for yourself?
4. Does it make you feel good to buy things for yourself or others, even if you're not sure you have enough money to pay for them?
5. If your significant other hasn't bought you anything special in some time, do you wonder whether he or she still loves you?

If you answered "yes" to three or more questions, then you believe at least partially in the myth that money equals love.

Exercises to Debunk "Money = Love"

If you subscribe to this myth in your actions and attitudes, spend some time thinking about people who don't fit the model. How about that friend from high school whose parents gave him a huge allowance, a credit card, a car, a top-of-the-line laptop, phone, and so on, but were always too busy to spend time with him? He had money, but he may have been starved for love.

Now consider the flip side: people without much money who have a lot of love in their life. We seldom hear about them because they're not celebrities, but they're all around us: neighbors, teachers, ministers, and certainly a great number of parents.

To reeducate yourself about this myth, you need to develop ways of making yourself feel loved and valued that don't involve spending money. For example, instead of shopping (online or off), you might get together with a good friend whose support makes you feel nurtured. Or make plans for an activity you can look forward to: Skyping with your little nephew, say, or going to a movie with your partner or best buddy.

If the urge to spend sweeps over you like a tidal wave, you may have a spending addiction. This condition usually results from a combination of early childhood deprivation (on an emotional, physical, or material level) and loneliness stemming from our society's lack of community, family dispersion, and feelings of spiritual emptiness. Through spending, we try to fulfill our craving to feel whole on some level.

If you are struggling with what feels like an addiction or a compulsion to spend, there's no need to be ashamed of it. A free 12-step program such as Debtors Anonymous (see Further Resources) can offer invaluable assistance.

The big problem with using money as a substitute for love is that it doesn't work. It's like putting a Band-Aid on a festering wound, temporarily covering over the feelings of loneliness, pain, or emptiness but never actually healing the wound. In fact, this "quick fix" can start a self-perpetuating downward spiral that leads to severe emotional and financial damage. By thinking of alternative activities that truly help us nurture ourselves, we can wean ourselves away from this pernicious myth.

Myth #3: Money Equals Power

Money = Power

The myth that "money equals power" is well entrenched in our society. Since we don't have kings, imams, or commissars running things, money has become the primary yardstick of power. There's no more striking example than the outsized compensation packages demanded by corporate chief executives. If Company A gives new hire John Doe a

$10 million salary plus $50 million in stock options, Richard Roe won't take the corner office at Company B for anything less than $15 million a year and $75 million in stock options. The question of whether these CEOs actually deliver that much value to shareholders and employees is usually never addressed. No wonder the villains in TV shows, movies, and novels are often corrupt, evil businesspeople motivated by greed! When we look around us, we see real-life examples of people who use their wealth and status to wield power over others. Money is a great aphrodisiac, and it's certainly true that wealthy men have used this power to attract women. On the positive side, money can give us more choices (for example, where to go to college and what kind of work to train for). It can enable us to travel, to live in a nice place, to eat well; it can buy good health care. And of course, the ability to make these choices is a kind of power. Still, freeing ourselves from the myth that money equals power can lead to new, creative life choices. Let's see how to make it happen.

DO YOU BELIEVE MONEY = POWER?

Which of the following statements seem true to you?
1. The most powerful people in the world are rich.
2. If I were wealthier, I would definitely be more powerful.
3. When people lose money, they lose power.
4. I need a lot of money to accomplish my goals and feel in control of my life.
5. With less money, I would have less power to live my life as I choose.

If you agree with three or more of these comments, the "money equals power" myth has a hold on you.

Exercises to Debunk "Money = Power"

Take a few minutes with pen and paper to think of people who disprove this money myth. First, jot down some examples of people who have (or had) a great deal of power without being wealthy. Numerous bad people with power aren't rich; consider Hitler, Stalin, or religious fanatics who urge their followers to murder others. But your list might also include people of modest means who have brought positive change to the world, such as Mother Teresa, who helped thousands of abandoned children in India; the Dalai Lama; and Abraham Lincoln, the Great Emancipator, not to mention countless scientists and inventors laboring on shoestring budgets who have rescued humanity from dread diseases and backbreaking toil.

After thinking about such examples, how would you answer these two questions?

- What factors other than money are required to gain the power to create a fulfilling life, accomplish one's goals, and maintain fulfilling relationships?
- On a scale of 1 to 10, how would you rate the importance of money and these other factors in helping you reach your goals?

We aren't saying it's wrong to become rich and powerful. Consider the many people who are wealthy, have power, and use them both for good. Members of this myth-busting group include Bono, the frontman of U2, who raises millions to fight hunger and poverty; the late Elizabeth Taylor, a dedicated AIDS activist; and Bill and Melinda Gates, whose Gates Foundation has given more than $28 billion to help people in the United States and around the world live healthier, more productive lives. There are many, many other folks who use money and power to improve the lives of others.

Remember, money can't buy the power that comes from being truly in harmony with your own values as you live your life. It can't buy happiness, friendship, or spiritual fulfillment. And all too often, what it costs is irreplaceable: time that could have been spent with loved ones, good health, personal fulfillment. In the end, true power is not power over others, but control over our own lives.[2] And many ways to achieve this control aren't determined by money.

Let's apply the idea of achieving personal power to your own situation:

- In what areas of life would you like to feel personally powerful?
- Which of these would require money? How much?
- How would it feel to achieve personal power? What words would describe it?

Myth #4: Money Equals Freedom

Money = Freedom

"Money equals freedom" is a myth that many of us hold dear. It gives us an excuse for not doing what we really want to do with our lives. We rationalize to ourselves, "If I just had more money, I would be free to paint, write that novel, travel to Europe, change careers..." or whatever we feel we were "meant" to do.

Remember, every money myth contains a grain of truth. Since it *does* cost money to do some of the things we want to do, we find it convenient to cling to this myth instead of finding out what really keeps us from the freedom we yearn for.

MONEY MYTHS

DO YOU BELIEVE MONEY = FREEDOM?

How many of the following comments do you agree with?
1. Lack of money is the main thing keeping me from what I really want to do.
2. If I won the lottery, I would be able to break free of my boring life.
3. Wealthy people have the freedom to create an ideal life.
4. The key to real freedom is having enough money.
5. I often think wistfully about all the things I could do, and all the freedom I would have, if I only had enough money.

You believe that money equals freedom, at least to some extent, if you answered "true" to three or more of these statements.

Exercises to Debunk "Money = Freedom"

To begin challenging the notion that money equals freedom, think of folks whose lives contradict this myth. Who do you know who has a lot of money but doesn't seem to be free at all? Perhaps it's a workaholic friend who repeatedly misses special family occasions, or someone who seems paralyzed by wealth they've inherited. On the other hand, there's a good chance you know one or more people who don't have a lot of money but seem very free. Many musicians, artists, writers, and self-employed people in other fields take pride in living lives uncluttered by a lot of financial baggage.

When the two of us were newly out of college, it was very much the thing to travel around Europe on the cheap. (The most popular travel book was *Europe on $5 a Day*, believe it or not.) Many of our friends hitchhiked around, staying in small villages as guests of people they met. They really got a sense of what each culture was like. It's hard not to contrast this experience with that of travelers who stay in expensive American-style hotels, never getting out and experiencing different lifestyles, or those who never travel at all because they have to stay home babysitting their portfolios. That doesn't seem like freedom at all.

By the way, we're not talking about the freedom to act out all our impulses, no matter how self-serving, rude, or destructive they may be. No amount of wealth makes that kind of freedom permissible. The freedom in question is the opportunity to reach our potential—to do and be what we wish.

Here's another exercise to help you debunk the "money equals freedom" myth:

- For two full weeks, keep track of what you spend your money on.
- On a scale of 1 to 10, rate how much pleasure each expenditure brings you.
- Note how much time you have to spend working to make the money to pay for these expenditures. (If you don't know your hourly rate, multiply the number of hours you work every week by 50, then divide that number into your annual salary. For example, 35 hours/week x 50 weeks = 1,750 hours/year. If you earn $45,500 a year: 45,500 ÷ 1,750 = $26.00/hour.)

This process can be revealing, for it may point out ways you are trading your free time to buy things you do not value or enjoy very much.

One last exercise: If you're willing to take a positive step toward your dreams and goals, think about the following:

- What can you do in the next six months that will give you more freedom, without requiring a major change in your financial situation?
- What has kept you from doing this up to now? Is it really money, or is it something else?

- In the next two weeks, how can you take a step toward the freedom you want?

If you do take action, remember to monitor your thoughts and feelings (at least in your mind) and reward yourself for moving in the direction of real freedom.

Myth #5: Money Equals Self-Worth

Money = Self-Worth

This myth tends to crop up when we think about how much we should be paid for our work. Self-employed people in particular often agonize over setting fees for their services: "How do I know how much I'm worth?"

Self-worth has nothing to do with the amount of money we're paid. More appropriate questions to ask ourselves might go something like this:

- "What's the going rate?"
- "How much do I need to make to cover my costs?"
- "How much feels right for me to charge?"
- "How much can I charge without feeling guilty or having an anxiety attack?" (Many of us have limits above which we are uncomfortable charging.)

The super-sized compensation demanded by company CEOs is an excellent example of equating self-worth with the size of one's paycheck: "Look at me! I'm paid the most, so I must be the best." Genetics and socialization combine to make men more prone to this competitive one-up, one-down viewpoint, but as greater numbers of women climb the corporate ladder, they too may become susceptible to measuring their self-worth by the money they make.

DO YOU BELIEVE MONEY = SELF-WORTH?

Would you agree or disagree with these comments?
1. I feel a lot better about myself when I'm making more money.
2. The net worth of other people affects how much I respect them.
3. If I earned less, people would look down on me.
4. If I lost my job, even for a short time, I would feel depressed, humiliated, and think less of myself.
5. If I found out that someone I knew was making a lot less than I thought, I would respect them less.

Did you agree with three or more statements? If so, you're a believer.

Exercises to Debunk "Money = Self-Worth"

Disproving this powerful myth begins (like the others we've debunked) with looking for examples that fly in its face. Think of people you know—or know of—who have a strong sense of self-confidence and self-esteem even though they aren't wealthy. Chances are, you've met a number of folks like this.

Then consider the other side of the coin: people who have a lot of money but very little sense of self-worth. Maybe they have trouble standing up for themselves, or are too quick to overmerge in relationships. Sometimes these folks try to compensate for feelings of unworthiness or insecurity by flaunting their wealth. We think you'll find many examples that show the myth of "money equals self-worth" just isn't true.

If your own feelings of self-worth are low because you don't make "enough" money, try this exercise:

- Imagine something you could do with your life that would not require a lot of money, but would make you feel more self-confident and proud of yourself.
- Write down a description of this activity or situation.

Bear in mind that you are under no pressure to take action right now. At some point in the future, you may feel ready to take a step toward making this happen.

If you are laid off unexpectedly, try to discourage yourself as quickly as possible from linking your lost income to your self-worth. Here's an example: Tina came in for therapy after learning that her job was being eliminated. Even though she hadn't enjoyed her work for the last two years and knew it was time to move on, she was stunned by the prospect of being jobless in a couple of weeks. Not only did the future scare her with its many unknowns, but the imminent loss of her salary was making her doubt her abilities and shaking the foundations of her self-esteem.

It took only a few sessions for Tina to disconnect her feelings of self-worth from this temporary trauma and start to recover her energy and passion. Within a month she was volunteering in a field she loved but had not had time to pursue. Within three months, she was offered a position in that new, more creative arena. The beginning salary was slightly lower than she had been paid before, but this had no effect on her self-esteem. Quite the contrary: doing something she loved greatly increased her confidence and her zest for life.

Since none of us have perfect parents, we go through life with holes in our psyches. We try to fill these holes with work (as in Tina's case), with other achievements, with possessions, and sometimes with bigger and bigger amounts of money. But in the long run, others' admiration of our wealth can never fulfill us the same way our own self-respect will.

In short, the only way to truly enhance your self-esteem and self-worth is to fulfill your potential: to strive to do and be your best in the areas of life that inspire your passion and commitment. If you do, you'll keep growing and changing throughout your life in ways that make you feel more whole.

Myth #6: Money Equals Security

Money = Security

Even though many of us are spenders rather than savers, almost everyone subscribes to the myth that "money equals security" (especially in our later years). Starting with the introduction of 401(k) savings plans in the 1970s, we've been told that our security in retirement will depend on how much money we have. It's true, of course, that we need enough money to be sure we can take care of ourselves and our loved ones. But investing too much emotional energy in this money myth may be paralyzing and destructive.

Take David, for example. His uncle had attempted suicide after being bankrupted in a bad business deal. This had so traumatized David's father that he worried constantly about money and lectured his children on the evils of frivolous spending. When David himself became a lawyer, he worked day and night to save more and more money for retirement. Intent on providing himself and his wife with enough wealth to live comfortably and leave a substantial estate for their children, he refused to take any time off. He worked the night of his daughter's sixth-grade concert and his son's eighth-grade championship ball game, and criticized his wife for replacing a threadbare old couch with the "unnecessary luxury" of a new one.

At the age of 48, David had a serious heart attack that made him realize he was not safe and secure despite all his wealth. If he died, no matter how much money he left for his wife and young children, they would feel lost and unprotected. Gradually he began to adopt a more balanced worklife—one that let him spend more quality time with his loved ones and enjoy some of the money he had earned.

DO YOU BELIEVE MONEY = SECURITY?

To see whether this money myth has a grip on you, ask yourself these questions:

1. When you think you may not have saved enough money for the future, does it make you feel extremely worried?
2. Do you think people who spend a lot of money to indulge their immediate desires are unwise and shortsighted?
3. When you think about being comfortable and secure in your old age, is having enough money the main thing that comes to mind?

4. Does putting money away in "safe" investments give you a greater feeling of inner peace and security than anything else you might do?
5. If you are worried about your old age, does thinking about having plenty of money comfort you and allay most of your fears?

If you answered yes to three or more of these questions, you probably believe that money equals security.

Exercises to Debunk "Money = Security"

Here again, the beginning of deflating this myth is to find examples that contradict it. You know people, don't you, who are well-to-do but don't seem to feel secure? Sad to say, many widows are in this situation, fearing the future even though they were left with plenty of money. By the same token, you've almost surely met folks who feel very secure and confident about the future, despite not having a great deal of money.

What's the difference between these two sets of people? What does the "secure" group have that the other doesn't?

Michael Phillips, author of *The Seven Laws of Money* and other books, once told Olivia that when he looked around at older people he knew, wealth was not a major distinguishing factor of those who seemed truly secure. Instead, what differentiated these individuals was that they were surrounded by a supportive network of friends of all ages. They exchanged goods and services with these friends, who were glad to take them shopping, accompany them to the movies, or invite them to dinner. Michael's conclusion was that social connectedness, not money, is the most important ingredient in ensuring that one feels secure later in life.

65

A woman we'll call Helen is a good example. Helen had been left enough money by her late husband to live in a luxurious Florida retirement community. She disliked socializing and preferred to stay home smoking and watching TV, so she had no friends. She sometimes had to hire people to take her grocery shopping and help her with other chores, but because she was so judgmental about people, it was often hard to find and keep help.

Knowing she would be completely on her own in the event of an emergency, Helen did not feel secure even with her big trust fund. When she received a diagnosis of a slow-developing, deadly disease, she changed. For the first time she reached out to people. They responded with loving help and support, and when she died, she was not alone.

Granted, we do need to save for the years when we will no longer want (or perhaps be able) to work. But the realization that money is not security can dispel some of the anxiety about not having enough of it. Instead, we may be able to redirect this energy toward developing more satisfying and lasting personal relationships.

Your Third "Money Harmony" Assignment

It's time to assess the effect of the six money myths we have addressed:

Money = Happiness
Money = Love
Money = Power
Money = Freedom
Money = Self-Worth
Money = Security

For your final assignment in this chapter, answer these questions:

- Which money myths have had the most impact on your life? In what way?
- Have they affected your relationships with a partner, friends, parents, children, coworkers? If so, how?
- How would you like to change these beliefs and the attitudes and behaviors that stem from them?
- What one step could you take in the next two weeks to continue debunking the myths that prevent you from making rational decisions about your money?

Money does not equal any idealized human condition. Money equals dollars and cents, nothing more. It's simply a tool to help you attain some of your life goals. If you remember this, you will not be riddled with anxiety, guilt, fear, or shame about how to spend, save, or invest it. Instead, you'll be able to use your money in a way that satisfies your real needs and wants, and reflects your real values.

4.
YOUR MONEY TYPES:
DEALING WITH YOUR
MONEY PERSONALITY

In chapter 1, you took a quiz that gave you a general idea about which of five money personality types you tend to be: Hoarder, Spender, Money Monk, Avoider, or Amasser. In this chapter, we'll examine in detail the characteristics of each of these types as well as those of several other money types: Binger, Worrier, Risk Taker, and Risk Avoider.

These names are chosen to capture the essence of each type quickly and dramatically. Some folks have remarked on the negative connotations of the names. Hoarders, for example, have suggested in wounded tones, "Why don't you call us 'frugal' instead of 'hoarders'?" The answer is that we want to emphasize the tendency toward imbalance in each type. Why? Because it's when your money type is unbalanced enough to bother you or others around you that you have a problem.

Our discussions of each money type are designed to help you change the personality traits that may be causing you trouble, or at least to have more control over them. Thus, our focus will be on the weaknesses and problems characteristic of each type.

Remember, *most people are a mixture of types.* In the course of your money awareness work, you may even change types entirely. And if you are in a relationship, there may well be a shift to a new money type for one or both partners as you attempt to balance each other out (more about this in chapter 7).

In the next pages, you may choose to read about only the money type(s) you tend to personify. Or if you'd like to better understand the range of money types you might come in contact with, you may want to read about all of them.

Also, we'll be suggesting assignments that fall under the rubric of "doin' what doesn't come naturally." We recommend that you (1) choose your assignments from the suggested list or create them from your own imagination, (2) record your thoughts and feelings about new actions and attitudes that counter your usual tendencies, and (3) reward yourself for your new behavior. (But don't sabotage the process by choosing a reward that reinforces the behavior you wish to change.) In this way, you will get the maximum benefit from the chapter.

Of course, if being the money type(s) that you are is not a problem for you or for others you interact with, you need not do any of the related assignments. Just read and enjoy!

Hoarders Don't Spend Unless They Have To

The Money Hoarder

Money Hoarders, not surprisingly, like to save money. If you tend to be a Hoarder, you also like to prioritize your financial goals. You probably have a budget and may enjoy the process of creating a budget and adjusting it periodically.

You most likely have a hard time spending money on yourself and your loved ones, not just on luxury items but even on practical gifts.

Such purchases seem frivolous to you. You may also view spending on entertainment, vacations, and even clothing as largely unnecessary.

If you think about investing, you tend to be concerned with your future security, especially during retirement. "Saving for a rainy day" appeals to your orderly nature. Since being secure later in life is more important to you than buying things to enjoy now, you don't want to keep your money where it's easy to access. Some Hoarders hide cash in secret places instead of putting it in a bank, but these cases are relatively rare. Depending on how extreme your Hoarder tendencies are, you might exhibit some, most, or all of these traits.

If your hoarding does not cause you and your loved ones much angst or tension, you may not need to do anything about this way of spending (or should we say, *not* spending) money. Even though you feel to some degree that money equals security, this belief may work just fine for you—perhaps allowing you to accumulate a substantial nest egg, which should make life somewhat more worry-free.

However, if you sometimes feel too stingy, too worried, or too anxious to enjoy your money, you may want to consider practicing some new attitudes and actions that will help you alter this pattern. Especially if you find yourself in conflict with loved ones and friends over your frugal behavior, you may benefit from doing one or more of the suggested assignments. You'll stand a better chance of enjoying the benefits of your hoarding, without being overly constrained by it.

RONDA, THE WEALTHY HOARDER

Ronda loved saving money, to the point of becoming highly anxious when she had to spend it on anything. This was unusual, because she was quite wealthy. She had married a successful business owner and lived in a magnificent house inherited from her parents.

After Ronda, by then a widow, passed away, her daughter came home to organize and pack up her mother's possessions and papers.

Under Ronda's bed, she found boxes and boxes of coupons—all alphabetized, and some of them dating back years! This discovery was particularly bizarre, given that just a few steps away Ronda had stored thousands of dollars' worth of jewelry that her husband had bought her.

As we mentioned, most Hoarders subscribe to the "money equals security" myth. If you too are a strong believer in this myth, you may want to revisit the section in chapter 3 that deals with debunking it. This is the best way to develop a more flexible attitude.

Exercises For Hoarders

- Once a week, go out and spend money on an item you can enjoy right away. Choose something you wouldn't ordinarily allow yourself to buy.
- Once a week, buy a frivolous gift (something you would ordinarily see as a luxury) for someone you care about.
- Once a month, take some money ($25 or $50 is fine) that you were going to put into a savings or investment account, and instead spend it on yourself or a loved one.
- If you tend to consult a budget often, spend two weeks just trusting your instincts about what to buy. Then compare the results with your budget and see how this experiment went for you.

Spenders Love to Be Lavish with Money

The Spender

If you are a Spender, you like to buy things you can enjoy immediately. It probably pleases you to buy gifts for others, too. You may
spend most or all of the money you earn, and you may well be carrying a lot of debt. (Of course, not all people in debt are Spenders;
sometimes they simply have too little income to meet their funda-
mental living expenses.)

Spenders have a hard time saving and prioritizing their needs and
wants. This means it may be difficult for you to put aside enough
money for future expenditures and long-term goals. Chances are, you
also hate creating and following a budget. Most Spenders dislike the

very word *budget*; it makes them feel constrained, claustrophobic, and rebellious. (Tip: Think of it as a spending plan instead.)

Understandably, Spenders prefer to keep their money handy so they can spend it if they so desire. If they do invest, they probably lean toward choices that can be quickly liquidated. Putting their money in harder-to-access places like an IRA or 401(k) might help them keep their hands off it. In fact, choosing an investment vehicle that penalizes early or frequent withdrawals may signal that they are recovering overspenders.

Some Spenders tend to be aggressive investors, preferring to take risks in the hope of quick high returns instead of choosing more conservative investments for the long run. If their inability to defer gratification and save money makes them feel dissatisfied and concerned about the future, they may want to work with a financial advisor who is sensitive to their tendencies without being overly judgmental.

If you are an extreme Spender at the mercy of an addiction or compulsion, you may feel ashamed about your spending being out of control. Don't judge yourself too harshly. As we mentioned in chapter 2, it's not easy to stay sane and balanced in a culture that's all about consuming. For more help, see *Overcoming Overspending*, our book written specifically for Spenders and their partners.

CHARLENE, THE SHOPAHOLIC SPENDER

Whenever Charlene felt bored or a little low, she would go online, surfing from site to site until she found something to buy for herself or her children. She ran up huge credit card bills, but could seldom afford to pay more than the minimum due. This behavior continued for years, infuriating her husband.

When Charlene attended one of Olivia's workshops, she realized that she was unconsciously mimicking her mother's spending pattern. Her mom, a compulsive gambler who periodically ran deeply into debt, depended on her husband to bail her out. He would write a check to settle the debt, and she would promise contritely never to gamble again—till the next time. Charlene too would periodically come to her husband and confess, shamefaced, that she needed money to pay off what she owed. He would give her a check and tell her to curb her spending. She would promise to comply. Then she would be back online within days, surfing the Web for clothes, accessories, or gifts.

With the new awareness that she was following a family pattern, Charlene felt ready to take on her addictive spending tendencies once and for all. She joined Debtors Anonymous, consulted Olivia for short-term money therapy, and began rewarding herself in ways that were more satisfying than spending on short-term pleasures with money she didn't have.

Exercises For Spenders

- Decide how much money you want to save. Ask your bank to transfer that amount automatically once a month from your checking account into savings.
- Once a week, refrain from making one impulsive purchase.
- If you need to go shopping, go with a friend who is not a Spender. Tell him or her in advance the maximum amount you intend to spend on your purchases, and stick to this spending limit.
- Each time you spend money, write down the amount, the purpose, and your feelings about it (if feelings come up). At the end of a week, identify one major or minor change in your habits that will reduce your spending. Decide on something to do with your savings that will make you feel good about yourself.

DON'T BE SURPRISED BY AN EMOTIONAL BACKLASH

Out-of-control Spenders often have a big internal (and sometimes external) tantrum whenever they set limits on their spending behavior. It enrages them to be deprived of the freedom to buy anything they want, whenever they feel like it.

If you experience this emotional backlash, don't let it keep you from recommitting to the more balanced kind of money management you're striving for. You'll feel a boost in self-esteem and a greater sense of financial security. If you succeed in curbing your impulsive spending for weeks at a time, you can give yourself a more tangible reward—just not one that costs a lot of money or throws off your spending plan.

The Binger

Bingers are a volatile combination of Hoarders and Spenders. They save and save until some inner pressure becomes too great, and then they explode into a wild spending binge.

Bingers may seem quite normal while their spending is under control, but they never know when the next urge to splurge will hit. If a binge leads to serious overspending, it can overwhelm the Binger with massive debt. Like excessive Spenders, extreme Bingers need group support from organizations such as Debtors Anonymous.

HERMAN, THE BINGER

A typical Binger, Herman would save diligently for long periods of time, then impulsively spend thousands of dollars on a new car or entertainment system. If he didn't have enough money for these purchases, he would max out his credit cards or overdraw his checking account, even if it made his rent and utility checks bounce.

Herman's girlfriend felt jerked around by this erratic pattern of saving and spending. She finally persuaded him to take a hard look at the way he made these "decisions" to spend. (Actually they were more like attacks of fever, since he made his huge purchases in a trancelike state. All was calm for a while once they were over, but no one could predict when the next attack would come.)

Herman agreed to begin tracking his spending patterns and his feelings before and after going on a binge. He also wrote down his short-, medium-, and long-term goals to remind himself what his savings were for. The process taught him a great deal about his emotional responses to frustration, longing, deprivation, and stress. And as he began to understand how to head off the impulse to binge, he felt in charge of his money for the first time in his life.

COMPULSIVE BARGAIN HUNTERS

Compulsive bargain hunters are a particular type of Spender or Binger. Let Olivia tell you about an experience she once had as a guest on a TV talk show: "The theme was 'When a Tightwad Marries a Spendthrift,' and my role was to help several couples resolve their differences. However, one couple who came out onstage had a more extreme problem. Paul felt so compelled to buy bargains that he'd spent more than $5,000 on a snowmobile, even though he and his wife, Yvette, lived in an area where it hardly ever snowed! Why? 'Because it was on sale,' cracked Yvette. Though the audience had a good laugh, overspending was no joke for this couple. They had been forced to go to a credit counseling organization for help, and now Paul gave every paycheck to Yvette so she could begin paying off their substantial debt."

Exercises For Bingers

- The next time you feel the urge to binge, stop yourself. Instead, make a note of how you feel about *not* allowing yourself to spend. If possible, call a friend to talk about your feelings. Figure out what you could do to reward yourself for giving up this habitual behavior.
- If refraining from a binge is too difficult a step, slow down the process. Take stock of your feelings before and after the binge. Try to "choreograph" the process so you are more aware of what is happening. Note what you think the binge was supposed to accomplish, and whether or not it succeeded.
- Go to several meetings of Debtors Anonymous and see what help you can get from others struggling with similar spending issues. Find a DA group you like and feel comfortable with, and commit to weekly visits.

Worriers Are Anxious About Their Money

The Money Worrier

If you are a Money Worrier, you tend to be anxious about money all the time. You probably want to have a great deal of control over your finances. You may spend inordinate amounts of time checking your account balances online, balancing and rebalancing your checkbook, and worrying about where your money will come from and where it will go. You may spend a lot of energy envisioning all the things that could go wrong with your money or all the potential calamities that would require large amounts of money to fix.

In fact, money may well be the major preoccupation in your life. You probably believe that if you had a lot more of it, you could stop worrying. But if you are a true Worrier, nothing could be further from the truth. Having a lot more money would simply give you more to worry about. (Of course, if you are in the midst of a real financial crisis, such as losing your job, becoming ill, or having too little income to make ends meet, then worry may be an entirely appropriate stress response.)

Many Worriers are also Hoarders and Amassers, but it's possible to combine worrying with other money personality types. Olivia, for example, would characterize herself as a recovering Spender and Avoider who has fits of worrying, with a smattering of Money Monk that dates back to her hippie-activist days. Sherry is an Amasser with Hoarder tendencies who worries about overspending. Does that sound overwhelming and messy? Actually, it's interesting and challenging to work at balancing these types as we each progress in financial awareness.

GENEVIEVE, THE WORRIER

Fifty-year-old Genevieve was a chronic Money Worrier. Even if she and her husband were doing well in the family business, she still worried about money. She was forever reworking her budget and telling her children to watch their money, make sure no one took them for a ride financially, and so on.

When her father died and her ailing mother came to live with them, Genevieve felt so overwhelmed by this new burden and expense that she went into a deep, paralyzing depression. She was in no condition to find out what other sources of support existed, or to make sure her mother was well provided for.

When Genevieve came to see Olivia for money therapy, they worked on aspects of her chronic worrying for several months.

Genevieve learned to reach out to her husband, her friends, and the community around her for support. She began keeping a gratitude journal to focus on her blessings instead of her lacks. As her worrying slowly decreased, she felt better equipped to grapple with the difficult situation with her mother. Eventually she was able to find solutions, both financial and emotional, to help her whole family cope with the stress of caring for an elderly parent in failing health.

Exercises For Worriers

- Give yourself 15–30 minutes once a day to write down your money worries and think about them in an active, focused way. Try to schedule this "worry date" at the same time every day. (Doing it early in the morning will give you the rest of the day to train your consciousness away from money worry. But if you usually worry in the afternoon, choose that time of day instead.) Write what you will do (or what resources you will call on) if the worst happens.
- Try assigning alternate days to worrying and not worrying about money. For example, on Monday, Wednesday, and Friday, write down and reflect on your worries; reserve Tuesday, Thursday, Saturday, and Sunday for other things. Do you feel differently on "worry days" than on days you don't worry about money?
- Once a week for several weeks, consider the following questions:
  - What benefits do you think you get out of worrying about money?
  - Where did you learn how to worry about money so much?
  - What bad things might happen if you stopped worrying about money?
  - Where do you think these beliefs came from?

- o What would your life be like if you didn't worry about money?
- o What scares you about that scenario?
- o What would you like about it?

If you manage not to worry about money for a week, give yourself a reward (one that won't make you worry!).

The Money Avoider

If you're an Avoider, you probably tend not to balance your checkbook or pay bills promptly. You wait till the very last minute to do your taxes (or to send your tax preparer what she or he needs). You probably don't know how much money you have, how much you owe, or how much you spend, because you don't like budgeting or keeping financial records. Even if you have some money to invest, you may avoid doing anything with it because it seems like too much trouble.

What fuels this avoidance? Some Avoiders share with Money Monks the belief that money is dirty. Others have a kind of disdain for the boring, mundane details of their moneylife. ("Somebody else should be taking care of all this for me!") In still other cases, money management tasks make an Avoider feel overwhelmed or incompetent. Extreme Avoiders may even feel a kind of anxiety or paralysis, similar to math anxiety, about financial decision-making. By and large, most Avoiders believe they just aren't up to dealing with the complexities of managing money.

Both men and women can be Avoiders. But as we will see later on, moneyphobic women often act more overtly panicky, anxious, and helpless in the face of money tasks they'd rather avoid, whereas moneyphobic men in the same situation tend to appear more calm, cool, and collected. Women are quicker to admit feeling helpless and ashamed of their avoidance, whereas men's defenses allow them to act as if nothing is amiss. But both women and men will lose self-respect if their money avoidance continues unabated for too long.

Avoiders Go Through Life in the Dark About Money

If Avoiders are willing to face these uncomfortable feelings, a financial advisor may be able to help them decide how to handle their money and put their finances in order. But since an Avoider's natural tendency will be to hand over most of the decision-making (so they can keep avoiding it), it's crucial to find a trustworthy financial professional who feels comfortable assuming so much responsibility.

A much healthier solution for Avoiders would be to gradually take on more accountability for their own financial affairs, with their advisor's help and guidance. (We call these financial advisors "therapeutic educators"—they are committed to empowering their clients so that Avoiders don't remain in an oversurrendered, childlike mode.) As they learn more about money and investments, Avoiders in recovery will be able to determine how well certain financial options really serve their interests.

ELISE, THE AVOIDER

A typical Avoider, Elise was a victim of math anxiety in her early years. She later felt similar anxiety about managing her finances, so it was a relief when she married an older man who told her not to worry about money; he'd take care of everything. When he died suddenly, Elise was overwhelmed and in shock. Since she had no experience with money management, she was afraid of making terrible financial decisions and losing all the money her husband had left her. As a result she avoided making *any* decisions, and her feelings of inadequacy and shame caused her to avoid seeking help.

When she finally did visit a financial planner, she had an anxiety attack in his office while trying to fill out the initial information-gathering forms. The planner did one thing for her in that first session that Elise says she will never forget. He put his hands on her shoulders, looked into her eyes, and told her to relax and trust that she would have all the information and all the help she needed to make good decisions about her money. He also acknowledged her courage in seeking support, considering how much anxiety she felt about her financial affairs.

With this warm acceptance, Elise was finally able to relax. In a workshop years later, she confided that she had actually become quite competent in dealing with her money, and that everything was going well for her both emotionally and financially.

Exercises For Avoiders

- Once a week, address one aspect of your moneylife that you usually avoid (for example, set up a file-folder system for keeping track of your financial records).
- If you are procrastinating about a financial task, such as getting information together for taxes, set a time to do it and then *do it.* If you feel enormous resistance to doing this task, invite someone over to be there while you do it, or figure out a way of easing yourself into the task so that it is less unpleasant.
- If you usually wait a long time to pay bills, deal with them as soon as they arrive.
- Make a monthly date with yourself to learn about one aspect of your money, such as your mortgage, credit cards, or 401(k) investments, with guidance from reputable personal finance magazines or sites.
- If a financial task feels impossibly daunting, get help from a friend, loved one, or money professional. But don't neglect the guideline above: the more you learn, the more easily you can determine whether your advisor is truly helping you meet your goals.

Whether you choose one of these assignments or invent one of your own, remember to monitor your feelings about confronting something you usually avoid. Reward yourself for this new behavior— but not by avoiding another financial task!

To Money Monks, Money Is Dirty

The Money Monk

If you are a Money Monk, you believe having too much money will corrupt you. In general, you believe it's bad, dirty, and "the root of all evil." It stands to reason that you identify with people of modest means rather than with those who amass wealth. If you happen to come into a windfall somehow (through inheritance, for example), you tend to be uneasy or even anxious at the thought of the influx of so much money. You worry that you might "sell out," becoming greedier and more selfish and losing sight of your positive human, political, and/or spiritual ideals and values.

You probably avoid investing for fear that your money might grow and make you even wealthier. If you are willing to invest, you are most likely comfortable only with socially responsible investments that reflect your deeper values and convictions and that contribute to causes you would like to support.

SHARON, THE VIRTUOUS MONEY MONK

Educated in a Catholic school by nuns who instilled the virtues of living simply and rejecting materialism, Sharon was a typical Money Monk. She became an activist in the 1960s, going on peace marches, volunteering in soup kitchens, and sometimes even organizing demonstrations to oppose the Vietnam War and end poverty and homelessness. When she graduated from college in 1968, she went to work for a doctor she respected. After several years, he told her he was giving her a large raise. Sharon felt so overwhelmed by the amount of the raise that she began sabotaging herself at work. (In retrospect, she saw that this self-defeating behavior arose out of her anxiety about having too much money around.) Within several months of the raise, she quit and began working for a nonprofit organization that paid even less than her starting salary at the doctor's office. She felt like she was back on comfortable and familiar terrain—struggling to pay her bills, with nothing left over for personal pleasure and enjoyment.

Years later, in one of Olivia's workshops, Sharon realized that her choices and her ability to enjoy life had been limited by the conviction that money would corrupt her. Even though she never wanted to become a woman who was too wealthy (a "Jackie Onassis," as she described it), she now knew that she could enjoy her money more while still expressing her deeply held beliefs about American society and the "right way to live."

Exercises For Money Monks

- Spend money on yourself in a way that you have previously considered "selfish" or "decadent." Do you enjoy this new behavior at all?
- Imagine yourself coming into a large amount of money and *not* being corrupted by it. How would you feel? What would you do with this money?
- Conjure up examples, images, and memories of people you've known or read about who have a lot of money and are not corrupted by it—people who in fact do many things with their money that you admire and respect. What are your feelings about these people? What do you have in common with them?
- Think of people who are corrupt without being wealthy. Can you see that greed is not synonymous with wealth?

Amassers Are Obsessed with Growing Their Money

The Amasser

If you tend to be an Amasser, you are happiest when you have large amounts of money at your disposal. In fact, you may feel empty or not fully alive unless you are working hard to amass more money. It's a major challenge for you to cultivate life balance instead of constantly monitoring your money to be sure it's growing.

You may be called stingy, since you hate to spend money on anything you deem unnecessary or even contribute to charity. Maybe you tell your family and yourself that this will change when you reach your target number ("Honey, I promise we'll start taking vacations when my portfolio hits five million"). A lack of funds may lead to feelings of failure and even depression, since you tend to equate money with self-worth and power.

If you hire an investment advisor or financial planner, your major concern will be finding investments with high rates of return, since you hope to make as much money as you can as quickly as possible. You probably enjoy making your own financial decisions, so it may be quite difficult for you to give up much control to a financial professional.

If you tend to be a Worrier as well and are tired of being overly fixated on your money, you may actually welcome the opportunity to assign some of the details of your moneylife to a trustworthy financial advisor. However, you will need to learn how to tolerate market downturns without becoming panicked or angry with your advisor.

KEVIN, THE WORKAHOLIC AMASSER

Kevin, an Amasser, worked long hours to earn more money than he actually needed. In the evenings and on weekends, he spent hours at the computer monitoring his investments. Whenever he and his wife, Carrie, went on vacation, he made sure they stayed in places where he could flaunt how wealthy and successful he was. He bought Carrie expensive furs and jewels, and was proud of how classy she looked in them.

But even when he was supposed to be relaxing, he kept thinking and reading about how to increase his wealth. As the years went by, this obsession made him more and more boring to his friends and family. When Carrie finally decided to leave him, he asked her, stupefied, "How can you think about a divorce after all I've given you?"

She answered bitterly, "The way you ask that question proves you aren't here with me and haven't been for years. All you think about is money. I feel like a showpiece, not like someone you are sharing a life with. I want a real relationship with someone I can talk to."

After the shock of the divorce, Kevin began to understand the destructive effect of his money fixation. Realizing that he couldn't let money ruin his life, he devoted more time and energy in his next relationship to developing a real connection to his partner.

Exercises For Amassers

- Find a time—on a weekend, perhaps, or on vacation—when you can spend at least one day *not* dealing with money at all. You might want to practice this behavior for several weeks in a row, one day a week, and see if your feelings evolve in any way over time.
- Think about some of your dreams or goals for the future that don't require much (or any) money to attain and might lead to more solid emotional fulfillment. See if you can take steps toward one of these dreams or goals.
- Try to remember a time in your life when you were less preoccupied with money. What did that feel like? Did you like it? Did you dislike or fear it? Role-play having this attitude toward money for one day and see how you feel about it now.

Risk Takers and Risk Avoiders are the two remaining money types we'll talk about. Both are concerned primarily with investing styles. When two people are in a relationship, it's quite common for one partner to be a Risk Taker and the other a Risk Avoider, and for these opposing tendencies to be a source of friction. If you are in a relationship, do you and your partner fit this pattern?

Risk Takers Get High on the Thrill of the Ride

The Risk Taker

A Risk Taker tends to focus on the adage that "the greatest risks bring the greatest rewards," ignoring the possibility that they can also lead to the greatest losses. If you are a Risk Taker, you enjoy the adventure of taking a risk and riding the waves to what you hope will be a positive outcome. Safety and security feel like a straitjacket that limits your behavior and your financial options.

For many Risk Takers (who are usually male), the intense thrill of the ride is more important than reaching the destination. Acting on a hot tip from a friend or stockbroker, you may invest a lot of money in a single investment with hopes of hitting the jackpot. If your risk-taking behavior ends in financial loss, you tend to become extremely distressed and depressed.

Exercises For Risk Takers

- Take some money out of a high-risk investment and put it into a very safe one like a bank or credit union savings account. Leave it there for at least two weeks, and write down how this feels.
- Spend one whole week refraining from taking *any* financial risks. See if you can look for pleasure in other areas of your life.
- Think about and describe in detail, if possible, any memories or models from your childhood that may have influenced your growing up to be a Risk Taker.

When you perform one of these assignments or an exercise of your own choosing, you can expect to feel bored, frustrated, trapped—even depressed. Take our word for it that these feelings will pass. Eventually, operating in a more conservative mode will help you feel calmer and less stressed. If you're in a relationship with a comparative Risk Avoider, it should also be easier for the two of you to meet in the middle with new understanding, more intimacy, and a moderate, sane investment strategy.

Risk Avoiders Insist on Keeping Their Money Safe

The Risk Avoider

If you tend to be a Risk Avoider, you choose safety and security above all else in your financial affairs. You probably like to budget in order to avoid end-of-month "surprises." When you invest, you are happiest with low-risk investments, even though they yield low rewards. Having your money accessible isn't important to you; you invest with the goal of ensuring future security for yourself and your family.

Planning feels like contentment and security to Risk Avoiders (who are more likely to be women). By contrast, taking a financial risk feels like jumping off a cliff with a blindfold on, because you are certain it will end in catastrophe. You have a hard time imagining why anyone would enjoy risk-taking. You sure wouldn't!

Exercises For Risk Avoiders

- Once a week, take some financial action that seems risky to you, such as making a spontaneous purchase.
- In as much detail as possible, imagine taking a financial risk and having it pan out very well. Imagine all the feelings you would have about taking the risk and about the positive outcome. If one of your fantasies involves more financial risk than you are usually comfortable with, imagine what you could do to move closer to taking this risk, perhaps in a limited way.
- Consider taking $250 out of savings or another safe investment and putting it into a riskier investment that might yield higher returns. What are your feelings as you invest the money and as you wait for the financial outcome?
- Think about, and describe in detail if possible, why you've become a Risk Avoider. Were you influenced by a traumatic event or by the example of someone who was wiped out financially?

It may be *very* difficult for you to start taking risks with your money. You must accept it on faith that your anxious feelings will give way in time to a new sense of self-confidence and creativity as you increase your risk tolerance.

Remember: All Types Have Positive Qualities

Now that you have completed your review of the basic money types with their limitations and tendencies toward imbalance, we want to reemphasize that each type has positive attributes.

Hoarders are good at budgeting, prioritizing, and delaying gratification. Spenders are generous with themselves and others, and know how to enjoy life in the moment. Money Monks have a high degree of moral integrity and are committed to noble ideals. Amassers understand the benefits of money in many different ways. Worriers are usually responsible about money and do well at keeping track of their finances. Avoiders don't let money take up too much space in their lives and are often creatively and constructively involved in other activities and passions. Risk Takers know the value of risk, and Risk Avoiders know the value of safety.

Your Fourth "Money Harmony" Assignment

Whatever combination of money types you tend to be, you'll profit from identifying all the attitudes and behaviors that you would like to change, as well as the best ways of making these changes. Based on what you have learned so far, spend some time thinking about the following questions and jotting down your answers:

- Are any money personality traits causing problems for you in some way?
- Which traits create tension in your relationships?
- Which traits seem to be the most ingrained or inflexible?
- In general, do you want to change your behavior, your underlying attitudes, or both?
- Which negative traits or chronic patterns are you willing to confront directly by "practicing the nonhabitual" over a period of time?

- When learning to do what doesn't come naturally, is it easier for you to work on your attitudes or to adopt behaviors unlike your usual money type?
- What kinds of rewards do you find are best to reinforce new behavior?
- What is the best way for you to monitor your reaction to new behaviors and track your progress? Does it work better to record your feelings, or to close your eyes and visualize how you feel when you practice these new actions or try on new attitudes? Would drawing pictures about your reactions be useful to you?

As you notice more and more about yourself over time, you can make adjustments, some subtle and some dramatic, so that your money personality becomes a blend of styles that suits you well, free of extreme imbalances or compulsions.

In the next chapter on money dialogues, you will learn to practice the most effective exercise we know of for getting at—and transforming—your core issues and conflicts in connection with money.

5.
MONEY DIALOGUES: TOOLS FOR GROWTH AND TRANSFORMATION

When you're trying to assess the relationship between your money and yourself, it's often hard to gain the perspective you need. Years ago, Olivia helped resolve this dilemma by introducing the "money dialogue," an insight-producing exercise that has proved of immense assistance to people who want to understand themselves better. Here's how she describes its genesis and value:

"When I first began teaching men and women about money harmony, I feared that people might react negatively to my Idea that we all have a relationship with money analogous to a relationship with a person. Yet I believed that if we used this metaphor to explore aspects of our relationship with money (for example, its current status, the major past influences, the changes that need to be made), we could discover an amazing array of irrationalities that block us from using money wisely.

"So I took an old gestalt therapy exercise and fashioned it into an assignment I called a money dialogue. But still I had doubts: would people find this exercise too weird and kinky? Would anyone, except maybe a few uninhibited individuals, be able to create a money dialogue with the proper degree of spontaneity?

"Happily, my fears were groundless. Most of my clients have been willing to create money dialogues, and have gleaned a tremendous amount of information from them. Some have told me the assignment was actually fun! After reading and hearing hundreds of these dialogues, I must say (to adapt a famous quote by Will Rogers), 'I never met a money dialogue I didn't like.' They are always revealing and often funny, touching, and profound."

What Money Dialogues Look Like

MONEY DIALOGUES

As the next step in moving toward money harmony, we invite you to create one or more money dialogues of your own. You're likely to learn new things about yourself—and you may find the process as creative and enjoyable as many others have.

How to Create a Money Dialogue

Let's begin by supposing that Money is a person with whom you are having a relationship. Imagine having a conversation with Money about how your relationship is going. If this seems hard to do, try imagining that Money is being interviewed on a talk show. What would Money say about how you are treating him/her/it? For example, if you are a Spender, Money might say, "He throws me around; he doesn't treat me with respect." If you are a Hoarder, Money might complain, "She holds on to me so tight, I can't breathe!" If you are a Money Monk, Money might remark, "He thinks I'm dirty. What a self-righteous guy!" When you conjure up this funny picture of Money being interviewed on a talk show, it becomes easier for you to visualize Money as a person with whom you are actually having a relationship.

Now let's create a dialogue with Money by talking to it (him/her) directly. (It's best to write down or record this dialogue so you can review it later.) Here are five steps to follow for preparing not only the dialogue but also an "internal commentary" on it:

1. Have a conversation with Money about how the relationship is going. The length of the conversation is up to you. Just go at your own pace, and let it continue until you feel it winding down of its own accord. Let yourself be surprised by what emerges. If a picture of what Money looks like comes into your head, draw it or describe how Money appears to you.
2. Have your mother (the voice of your mother in your head, that is) comment as if she has just finished reading the dialogue

you've written. This commentary should be quite brief—a sentence or two, or a short paragraph at most.

3. Have your father comment on the dialogue. Sometimes fathers (or mothers) have no comment at all and respond with silence. Of course, that's significant too. But if you can imagine what Dad would be thinking after reading your money dialogue, have him say it—even if he wouldn't say it aloud in real life.

4. Allow any other powerful influences from the past to comment on your money dialogue. It could be a spouse, or if you are divorced, your ex-spouse might have something to say. Or your grandmother or grandfather, a godparent, a religious teacher, your best friend—anyone who influenced your relationship with money.

5. Finally, have God, or your Higher Power, or your voice of inner wisdom comment on the dialogue you've written.

If you have trouble creating this conversation and are feeling stuck, you'll find inspiration in the sample money dialogues of a Spender, Hoarder, Avoider, Money Monk, and Amasser that follow in this chapter. But if possible, create your own dialogue first and read the sample dialogues later.

Olivia's Money Dialogue: A Spender's World

Here's the first money dialogue Olivia wrote as a recovering overspender:

MONEY: You never seem to be able to hold on to me long enough to satisfy your important long-range goals. What's your problem?

OLIVIA: I feel alive and happy only when I'm spending you. When I'm not spending you, I feel deprived, empty, depressed.

MONEY: That's seeing only one side of what I can do for you. You're like a spoiled kid who can't wait for anything she wants.

OLIVIA: It's true; I know how to indulge myself in my whims, but not how to treat myself well in the deepest sense. So instead of attacking me, how about helping me with this?

MONEY: It's not in my power to do that. I'm just a bunch of dollars and cents. Maybe your husband, friends, or a therapist could help you with how you deal with me. Frankly, I'm at a loss.

OLIVIA: Maybe if I could focus on my long-term money needs and goals, I could save you more for future security, travel, and my son's education. And maybe I could explore new ways to nurture myself, instead of running out and buying clothing when I feel blue or want to celebrate.

MONEY: Sounds good to me. Just please try to throw me around less and show me a little respect.

OLIVIA: I'll try.

OLIVIA'S INTERNAL COMMENTARY

HER HUSBAND: Pay off your credit cards every month. If you can't, talk to me so I can help you. And be sure to put away some of your income for taxes and retirement.

MOM: Why not indulge yourself as I did? Life is short, and it's too bad you and I didn't find men who could give us all we really wanted. On the other hand, you *are* kind of a spoiled brat and need to learn some self-control!

DAD: I think you're doing okay, dear, but I worry about your future security. Like Mom, I'm sorry you didn't find a rich husband to take care of all this for you.

GOD: Sorry your parents don't have the advice you need to hear. But you're on the right track. It makes sense to follow your husband's good advice about money. And pursuing your deeper, real needs is definitely the way to stop your over-spending. The more you love yourself and increase your self-esteem, the more likely it is that money will assume its proper perspective.

Notice that Olivia didn't include comments from anyone other than her husband, Mom, Dad, and God. That's because their powerful voices were the only ones she heard.

Fred's Money Dialogue: A Hoarder's World

Fred's father came from a large family where there was never enough money. Emulating his dad's fears and behavior with money, Fred became a Hoarder. His wife, Marie, and his kids complain constantly about his extreme hoarding tendencies.

MONEY: You never take me anywhere. You hold on to me so tight, I'm getting squeezed to death!

FRED: I'm so afraid that if I spend you, you'll disappear altogether. My dad told me we could lose everything unless we were extremely careful with every penny, and I believed him.

MONEY: How long are you gonna keep living as if you're in dire straits? You make good money now, and you don't enjoy it at all.

FRED: But what about security for the future? Don't I have to start saving now for my old age?

MONEY: Yes, but not as extremely and compulsively as you do. Look at the stress it causes in your marriage, and notice how guilty and stingy you feel inside. Why, you're so tight they call you "Squeak"!

FRED: It's true, I don't like it much. But I'm afraid that if I change and loosen up at all, I'll lose everything.

MONEY: Oh brother, are you a tough case!

FRED'S INTERNAL COMMENTARY

DAD: You're right, son! You can never have too much money in the bank or too much security for the future. Don't let money seduce you into foolishness. You never know when the ground might get shaky under your feet. You have to be prepared for the worst.

MOM: Well, dear, as long as you're making a good living, I don't see why you have to worry that much... though your dad *is* usually right about these things. Even though we never had many frills, we didn't starve, either. I'm grateful that your dad was such a hard worker, and that he was never frivolous with our money. We went without meals sometimes so that we could manage to send you kids to college and grad school, and I'm proud we were able to do all that.

MARIE: I can't stand listening to you talk about money. Your constant hoarding and worrying make me want to scream! As long as you keep being so tight, I'll keep spending to get back at you and squirreling money away on the sly.

HIGHER POWER: It's time to experiment with giving in to more spontaneity and pleasure. You can trust yourself that if you do, you won't go overboard and become a crazy overspender. You are wise enough to find true balance if you begin practicing trust and relaxation. Just start in small increments and then slowly expand your capacity to spend some money for things you can enjoy now.

Myrna's Money Dialogue: An Avoider's World

Myrna, an Avoider, has such intense money anxiety that she puts off all financial dealings till the last possible moment. This extreme avoidance exasperated her ex-husband, Paul, and contributed to the breakup of her marriage.

MONEY: Why do you always avoid dealing with me? You treat me like a leper!

MYRNA: You make me feel incompetent and helpless. I'd prefer *never* having to deal with you!

MONEY: That's not my fault. And the more you avoid me, the more of a pain in the neck I become. I can't go away altogether. You need me to function.

MYRNA: I know, and I resent that terribly. I just wish someone else in my life would take care of you for me.

MONEY: Sorry, but there's no one around who will. What makes dealing with me so awful? I'm not a monster, you know—just dollars and cents.

MYRNA: No one ever taught me about how to treat you, how to take care of you. I don't know how to begin.

MONEY: One step at a time. There are others around who could help you, you know. They just can't rescue you. Once you start paying some more attention to me, you'll see I'm not such a bad guy after all. I just don't like to be ignored.

MYRNA'S INTERNAL COMMENTARY

MOM: I always told you that you were incompetent around money, just like your dad. I hope you hire someone else to handle your money for you. You'll *never* be able to do it yourself!

DAD: I never had a head for figures. Other things were more important to me. People were my strong suit. Luckily, your mom took care of the whole thing for me. She was good at managing money. But she made me feel like a worm for not being able to do it myself.

PAUL: Grow up and begin taking responsibility for yourself. Otherwise, no man will put up with your extreme helplessness. I sure couldn't!

GOD: Forgive yourself for your fears and avoidance. I've already forgiven you. If you start taking small steps to handle money tasks you usually avoid, while tolerating your uncomfortable feelings about money, you will get the job done. The sooner you start, the quicker your self-esteem will rise. Once you start exercising your own muscles, you will have all the help you need to get the job done. Money will then feel like a friend, rather than a source of anxiety and fear.

Ricky's Money Dialogue: A Money Monk's World

Ricky is a typical Money Monk. Taught in a religious school that money was evil, he later became an activist who vowed never to be identified with "those corrupt wealthy schmucks in the military-industrial complex." His dialogue clearly illustrates his mind-set:

MONEY: You act like I'm the devil or something. The way you back away from me in horror makes no sense!

RICKY: I gotta make sure I don't have too much of you around or I risk selling out, becoming bourgeois, fat, and lazy—if not downright greedy and corrupt.

MONEY: I don't have the power to corrupt you. Some people have a lot of me and treat me well. We have a good time together, and we don't do anyone any harm.

RICKY: Yeah? Name two people you know who are like that. All the people I respect are struggling financially just as I am. They know the value of a dollar, and they know it's better not to get too comfortable and smug.

MONEY: What about all the good that Bill Gates and Warren Buffett do with their money? And look at how simply Mr. Buffett lives! Boy, I hope you open your eyes before it's too late. Otherwise, our war will just escalate over time—from your end, I mean. Grow up, kiddo; you don't have to suffer to be virtuous.

RICKY: I'll think about that... though I still don't trust you. Maybe all this is just a con.

RICKY'S INTERNAL COMMENTARY

MOM: Honey, you really don't have to deny yourself so many comforts. Now that I'm getting older, I wish your life were a little easier materially and in other ways.

DAD: Son, I'm proud that you've stayed such a simple person in the midst of this world of corruption. Don't give in; keep resisting temptation in the form of money.

FATHER LUKE: Waste not, want not, my son. Don't give in to the seduction of money and things. Live simply, and live by your true spiritual values of simplicity and self-sacrifice.

GOD: There is no need to starve yourself so that others may eat. Look for examples all around you of those who have money and use it well. It might be more creative and enlightening for you to experience having money and using it well to reflect your deepest values, than to make sure you keep it far away from you.

Arlene's Money Dialogue: An Amasser's World

Arlene is an Amasser from a poor family. Her parents separated when she was young, and her mother struggled to support her and her three siblings. As a child, Arlene was constantly subjected to her mother's bitterness about her father's failure to make a good living and pay child support. Arlene vowed never to be as poor and desperate as her overworked mother. She found a role model in her aunt Irene, who owned a dress shop and worked constantly to earn money until she was able to marry a wealthy lawyer.

MONEY DIALOGUES

MONEY: Boy, you pay me so much attention, sometimes I just wish you'd give me a rest!

ARLENE: I can never get enough of you to relax and feel satisfied. The more of you I have around at all times, the happier and safer I feel.

MONEY: Yeah, but I'm getting exhausted from being constantly saved, invested, reinvested, flaunted, and on and on. I mean, I like *some* attention, but this is ridiculous.

ARLENE: With you around, I feel I'm worth something... that others will respect me and not put me down. Maybe I can even use you to find a rich husband so I'll have more of you around. I wouldn't mind working less and still enjoying you more and more.

MONEY: Not only are you obsessed, but you want something for nothing. It's a dangerous trip, my girl!

ARLENE: Well, I'm not ready to give it up—not until I have at least a few million of you around. Then I'll *think* about it. And you work for me, not the other way around. Remember that, buddy!

MONEY: Some "buddy"!

ARLENE'S INTERNAL COMMENTARY

MOTHER: Stick to your guns, kid. I wish I were as good as you are at getting money in large quantities. Then I wouldn't have had to struggle and feel like a nobody.

DAD: Your mother and you are both crass materialists of the worst kind. I'm glad I got away from the two of you. Money isn't everything, you know. I had a much happier life than your mom, and I still don't have a lot of money.

AUNT IRENE: I hope you end up wealthier than all the men in your life. If you have enough money, you don't need people much. Of course, if you are lucky enough to find a rich husband as I did, so much the better!

INNER VOICE: It's time to look at what's driving you so hard about getting more and more money. It will never make up for your years of deprivation and struggle with your mother, or for the lack of fathering in your childhood. If you get money down to its proper role in your life, you will be able to relax and enjoy yourself. Otherwise, you will feel you never have enough of it, and you will continue to be driven by, and sacrifice relationships to, this pursuit of money. Love yourself a little more, and worship money a little less.

Writing Your Own Money Dialogue

What will your own dialogue tell you? First, it will give you a more in-depth picture of how your life with money is really going, what sticking points or conflicts are involved, and what your strengths and weaknesses are. Second, it will give you a better handle on what influences from your past formed your money personality. Finally, through the voice of God (or your Higher Power, or inner wisdom), it will help you see what direction you need to move in, as well as a step you can take or an attitude you can adopt to evolve toward more harmony in your moneylife.

Sometimes Money itself functions as a kind of inner wisdom or Higher Power in the dialogue. That's fine, too. There are no wrong ways to do a money dialogue. Whatever you come up with will help you become more aware of yourself, your money, and what money harmony would look like for you.

Your Fifth Money Harmony Assignment

Have you created your own money dialogue yet? If you haven't, and you're willing to imagine a conversation with Money followed by the commentary of your parents, other influences, and the voice of God, write one now. Ready, set, go!

What You Can Learn from Your Money Dialogue

What strikes you most strongly about your own money dialogue? What have you learned or been reminded of, or what has affected you emotionally? What insights has it given you that may help in your search for balance in your moneylife? Has it led you to any ideas about the next step in practicing the nonhabitual?

Money dialogues can (and ideally should) be done again and again. Each time, your dialogue will evolve a little as your relationship with money becomes clearer and more conscious. If you tune in to your own sense of timing, you'll know whether to do these dialogues once a month, every other week, once a week, or every day for a week. In any case, creating money dialogues periodically will help you track your movement toward money harmony and, little by little, remove the blocks along the way. You can also do a targeted money dialogue about a particular money conflict or issue you are grappling with.

The money dialogue is a powerful assignment. Do not underestimate its power to shake loose old dysfunctional attitudes and behaviors and to move you toward balance in your moneylife. By paying attention to the insights gleaned from your dialogue and following through on them, you are taking responsibility for turning your relationship with money into one that fulfills your real needs.

With the creation of your own money dialogue, you have completed the first half of your journey toward money harmony. Now you are ready to begin looking at differences between men and women in the area of money.

PART TWO

MONEY HARMONY FOR YOU AND YOUR PARTNER

6.
MALE-FEMALE DIFFERENCES AROUND MONEY: UNDERSTANDING TWO DIFFERENT CULTURES

The longest-running solo play on Broadway is comedian Rob Becker's *Defending the Caveman,* a brilliant, hilarious analysis of differences between men and women. The premise of his routine is that most of these differences stem from caveman times, when men were raised to be hunters and women learned to be gatherers. Male hunters focused on one thing and one thing only—the rear of the animal to be killed—and performed this primary survival task in silence. A man gained status in the community by killing more animals than the other men did. Female gatherers, on the other hand, chitchatted with their women friends as they went to the fields to gather berries, medicinal herbs, and so on, in cooperative harmony.

Becker dramatizes a number of ways in which these differences cause problems today for men and women in couple relationships. Take shopping, for instance: men go to a store, "kill" the shirt they need, wear it till it dies, then go "kill" another one. Women roam the mall, "gathering" gifts for themselves and their loved ones: a book for their niece, a tie for their husband, an outfit for a friend's new baby.

To illustrate how men tend to compete and women tend to cooperate, Becker acts out the different scenarios when groups of men or women are standing around an empty potato chip bowl at a party. Women go as a group to replace the chips, chatting all the while and never missing a beat. Men negotiate among themselves about who will refill the bowl, with each man trying to avoid the task. The loser has to replace the chips. Unless women step in and refill the bowl themselves, all conversation will have broken down by then.

The show is a riot. Audiences laugh until their sides hurt, eyeing each other as they recognize themselves and their mates. Behind this laughter is the healing realization that many male/female conflicts stem from our upbringing to perform different roles in life, and that the sexes' different worldviews reflect these divergent roles. In recent years, we have also learned from neuroscience research that some differences may be hardwired in the womb.

In this chapter, we'll look at differences in how men and women think and act around money. Neither view is "right" or "wrong," of course. In fact, we believe it's best to adopt an attitude of detachment and curiosity as you read, as if women and men were coming from two completely disparate cultures—perhaps Mars and Venus, as John Gray suggests. It will also help if, like Rob Becker, you can see the humor in the differences between the sexes.

A caution: Although many of these attitudes and behaviors seem gender-specific, there are a great many exceptions for every supposed "rule" comparing men and women. So if the shoe doesn't fit, don't try to wear it!

Overcoming Money Differences Together

That said, we believe that if you reflect on the wide range of gender differences, from perceptions and experiences to investment and communication styles, you will find it easier to empathize with your own loved one(s) of the opposite sex. This in turn will help create a positive and respectful climate for your moneytalks.

Differences in Brain Wiring

Today, we're just beginning to learn how many gender differences are hardwired. Kathleen Burns Kingsbury, a wealth psychology specialist and author, brings together gender-related findings from a number of respected brain experts in *How to Give Financial Advice to Women: Attracting and Retaining High-Net-Worth Female Clients.* One of Kingsbury's quotes, from *The Female Brain* by neuropsychiatrist Louann Brizendine, M.D., is particularly interesting: "Although male and female brains are 99% the same, the 1% gender difference in brain chemistry is evident in every cell of the body."

Dr. Brizendine's comment continues, "There is no unisex brain. [...] Girls arrive already wired as girls, and boys arrive already wired as boys. Their brains are different by the time they're born, and their brains are what drive their impulses, values and their reality."

Several physical differences in the brain tend to make women more relationship-oriented and more focused on caregiving, passing on legacies to the next generation, and using wealth to better the community. These differences involve three areas of the brain:

1. The amygdala and limbic system (center of emotion, fear, and aggression). The limbic system is larger in the female brain than in males'. Scientists hypothesize that this may contribute to women feeling responsible for caring for those they love, even at their own personal and financial expense.

2. The corpus callosum (connector that transmits signals between the left and right sides of the brain). Women have more connections between hemispheres, accounting for their proficiency in multitasking and verbal communication. Men's more limited number of connections makes them less verbal, but enables them to concentrate more fully on individual tasks. This difference between

his single focus and her more diffuse awareness often complicates moneytalks.

3. The hippocampus (hub of memory formation and recall). This too is larger in women than in men, perhaps accounting for women's greater ability to store and remember details.

As a corollary to the last point, men sometimes need to take more time to listen when women share details of their lives, choices, and goals. Most women appreciate it when their partner refers to specifics she has shared with him; it's an indicator of attentiveness and caring that can contribute to strengthening their relationship. Women who don't feel valued and listened to are more likely to react with coolness, turn away, or even end the relationship.

Differences in Socialization

If you're a guy growing up, the societal messages you get will probably be quite different from those that girls receive. The six differences below will have a profound effect on your behavior and attitudes toward money.

1. SOLID BOUNDARIES VS. FLUID BOUNDARIES

To grow into a normal adult, a child must separate from his or her mother (usually the primary caregiver) and develop a sense of personal boundaries. It's crucial for boys to differentiate themselves from their parent of the opposite sex, so they develop more solid—sometimes even rigid—personal boundaries. In later relationships, they tend to hold on to a separate sense of self. For girls, on the other hand, separating from their mother doesn't require such discrete boundaries. That's why women tend to be more comfortable with merging and connectedness in relationships.

2. "THINKING" VS. "FEELING" TYPES

Researchers working with the Myers-Briggs Type Personality Indicator have found that approximately six out of 10 men are thinking types, and six out of 10 women are feeling types.[3]

Using Carl Jung's terminology to describe the way people usually make decisions and resolve issues, Myers-Briggs identifies those who tend to be more objective, logical, and analytical as "thinking" types, whereas "feeling" types are more subjective, more empathetic, and more likely to strive for harmony.[4]

In most relationships, men and women choose mates of the opposite type. "Feelers" choose "thinkers" and vice versa in more than 90 percent of marriages, according to Bill Jeffries, a highly respected Myers-Briggs trainer. In Olivia's experience with client couples, it's most often the man who is more detached and analytical, and the woman who takes care of everyone's feelings and strives to maintain harmony in the relationship. This doesn't mean that "feeling" types are incapable of logic or that "thinking" types do not have strong emotions. We're merely describing ways in which these types tend to make decisions and move toward action.

3. COMPETITION VS. COOPERATION

In general, women are brought up to avoid conflict, to be "nice," giving to others and accommodating their needs—in short, to seek cooperation and harmony. Men are more often raised to compete assertively and aggressively in order to win power and position. They see the world as hierarchical: I'm up, you're down.[5]

Most men do learn to function as team players in sports or the workplace, but they still tend to view the world in the context of competition and hierarchy. Thus, they may need to feel one-up in an intimate relationship if they think the only alternative is to be one-down to their mate. This competitive/cooperative difference will influence how a man and woman talk about money and who makes the major financial decisions.

4. VULNERABILITY VS. INVINCIBILITY

Because women are socialized to play well with others, they are relatively comfortable expressing their feelings. Sharing their own shortcomings with someone else is a gesture of friendliness and trust. But to a guy raised to compete and win, admitting to weakness or neediness is unacceptably wimpy, unmanly, and shameful. The upshot is that women have a hard time claiming their strengths with money, and men sometimes can't own up to their weak spots.

5. SELF-CONFIDENCE VS. DOUBT

In spite of societal changes over the last 50 years, many girls still grow up in the conscious or unconscious belief that dealing with finances is a man's job. For example, both of Olivia's parents (who often told her she could do anything she set her mind to) made it clear that she wouldn't be good at "this money stuff." They told her, "If you're lucky, you'll find some rich guy to marry you and take care of you." Even though a perfect SAT score in math gave her no reason to doubt her own abilities, she avoided dealing with taxes, investments, and other financial matters for years as a result of this early indoctrination.

And she was far from alone. The journey to engage women more fully with their money has been a long and, so far, not very successful one. Studies continue to show that women are less financially confident than men, despite decades of effort put into making them more comfortable with money and investing. It's encouraging that many younger women now believe they can be and do virtually anything they wish. Still, traditions die slowly—more slowly than many of us would like to admit—and the proportion of financially knowledgeable women has hardly budged. In fact, 2012 research by Financial Finesse indicates that the financial knowledge gap between men and women may be widening.[6]

For their part, men are expected to be proficient with money. It's something they're simply supposed to know, much like sex, without any education or experience. Since they've been socialized to hide any vulnerabilities, they often assume an air of financial authority that may or may not be justified. As Elizabeth Jetton, a Certified Financial Planner and former head of the Financial Planning Association, explained to us, "When I got into the business [at a brokerage firm], I knew nothing about investments. I just listened and observed, and I made an assumption that the men knew what they were doing. After being there a while, I realized that most of them did it in spite of how little they knew."

So when discussing money matters, two partners may display levels of confidence or insecurity that have little to do with their actual knowhow. Men feel they're expected to act authoritative about mortgages or mutual funds even if their actual knowledge is limited. By contrast, women tend to disclaim their expertise with money until they feel sure they know everything possible about it.

If these defenses are in place when they get together to talk about money as a couple, the woman typically seems emotional and anxious, while the man acts competent and in control (even if he really isn't). Only if both partners are willing to work with their own defenses can they remove these "masks" and deal with the issues at hand.

6. TAKING CREDIT VS. ASSUMING BLAME

These differences cause men and women to react to financial success and failure in opposite ways. It's most obvious if they work with an investment advisor. When men's investments are doing well, they tend to credit their own financial acumen. When they lose money, they tend to blame the advisor, bad luck, or fate. That's not surprising, since they've been raised to be winners and hide their weaknesses.

By contrast, when women's investments are up, they credit good luck, good timing, or good advice. When they lose money, they blame themselves. This too is understandable, since women are socialized not to assert their own capability but to express vulnerability and dependency on others.

Although these attitudes are buried deep in our DNA, they can be overcome with awareness, education, and hard work. We need to be focused and vigilant in creating an environment where men and women can overcome their programming to live in a way that reflects their own unique individuality and their values. When we no longer see ourselves as slaves of our genes and our upbringing, we can exercise choice in a way that fulfills us and our loved ones.

Different Communication Styles

When Deborah Tannen, a professor of linguistics at Georgetown University, explored the ways each sex uses language for her pioneering book *You Just Don't Understand: Women and Men in Conversation*, she was overwhelmed by the differences separating females and males at every age. Even the second-grade girls she studied were more similar to adult women in their use of language than they were to boys of their own age.

This relates to the different ways that emotions are handled. When adolescent girls experience negative emotions such as anger, humiliation, or sadness, much of the brain activity associated with their feelings moves to the cerebral cortex, an area connected with such functions as reflection, reasoning, and language. In boys, negative emotions remain in the amygdala, the "fight or flight" part of the brain. This may explain why men tend to react more quickly and explosively to negative emotions, while women are more likely to discuss and process their feelings. When it comes to money, these different ways of handling emotion can quickly turn a conversation into a conflict.

Communication may be further complicated when men and women start a moneytalk with different expectations. These stem from many of the major differences between the genders: hunter versus gatherer, competition versus cooperation, thinking type versus feeling type.[7] "Thinking type" men sometimes complain that women resist discussing nitty-gritty aspects of the family finances. "Feeling type" women, on the other hand, complain about men's resistance to dealing with personal dynamics and emotional issues.

Hurt, misunderstanding, and conflict can result from these disparate communication styles:

- Most women need to be empathetically heard and emotionally understood. But when she shares her feelings, he may discourage or criticize her for burdening him with "unnecessary" information. For example, she may want to talk about ways that the two of them are not sharing power, or discuss her yearnings about what to do with their money, when all he wants to discuss is refinancing the mortgage.

- A man often responds to a complicated or emotionally fraught issue with a rational analysis and prompt advice, assuming that a quick solution is what his partner wants. In this hunter mode, he doesn't recognize that she is still trying to "gather" all the different aspects of the issue to share. So when he interrupts in an attempt to kill the problem for her, she may feel patronized, ignored or lectured at, and disrespected.

We suggest that "ladies first" makes sense in a situation like this. Begin by discussing feelings and dynamics, then move on to hard facts. Only after feelings are expressed and received, lightening the emotional weight, can the facts be aired and heard and useful negotiations ensue.

LOOK AT ME (OR DON'T)

When having a discussion about something important, women consider it important to be physically or at least visually connected: making eye contact, talking directly to their partner, or even touching each other. By contrast, men often feel more comfortable when not making eye contact, and would rather sit side by side in a conversation than face-to-face.

DON'T BLAME ME!

In discussing earlier how men and women react to financial success and failure, we saw that men tend to take the credit and brush off the blame, whereas women are more likely to take the blame and brush off the credit. Consequently, the tendency in arguments about money is for him to blame her and for her to blame herself.

Sometimes the blame game is evenly matched, with each partner trying to pin the blame on the other. With other couples, the man may be more verbally abusive and physically explosive; occasionally the woman is the attacker, wielding sharp-tongued criticism. No matter who "wins," the dynamic tends to go like this:

PARTNER 1: It's your fault we have no money. Look at the crazy things you spend it on!

PARTNER 2 (defensively): Okay, okay. I guess I *am* a little reckless and impulsive.

But the cycle won't end there. The individual who is one-down in this conflict will begin harboring more and more resentment toward the partner who made him or her feel blamed and wronged. Ultimately, this resentment will transform into getting even in any of a variety of ways: being critical, acting cold and distant, withholding sex, or spending more money, overtly or in secret.

To avoid hostile dynamics that leave hurts, grudges, and bitterness in their wake, it's crucial for both partners to minimize blame (and self-blame). Focus instead on your own part of the dynamic (which, after all, is the only part you have control of), and practice the ways to overcome destructive patterns that you're going to learn.

HOW DO YOU HEAL?

When a moneytalk gets heated and both partners feel too angry or hurt to continue, the woman will probably want to talk the problem out right then and there. The man would usually rather withdraw to get some space to heal. As John Gray puts it, he needs to "go into his cave" for a while.[8]

The only way to resolve this situation is for one person to surrender temporarily to the other's need. Either she has to give him a little space (it works best if he's willing to set a time frame on his withdrawal), or he has to tolerate his emotional discomfort while they try to solve their problem. The partner who gets to use his or her normal healing style might tell the other, "I realize you're stretching for the sake of our relationship, even though it may make you feel uncomfortable. That means a lot to me."

Different Ways of Learning

Given their differences in brain wiring, socialization, and communication styles, it's no surprise that men and women prefer to learn in different ways. One cue comes from 2004 research on chimpanzees in Tanzania, which found that female chimps tended to follow their teacher's example, while male chimps preferred to do things their own way. We naked apes may not be as evolutionarily superior as we like to think. Based on his classroom studies, psychologist and family physician Dr. Leonard Sax, author of *Why Gender Matters: What Parents and Teachers Need to Know About the Emerging Science of Sex Differences*, points out that boys are more likely than girls to consult their teacher only after all other options have been exhausted.

Women typically respond well to a small-group learning environment—for instance, a workshop or investment club. "Women are collaborators," explains Eleanor Blayney, a Certified Financial Planner and co-founder of Direction$, an organization that educates male and female financial advisors to understand and address women's needs. "Since the beginning of time, we've done our work in circles: quilting bees, sewing circles, and so on. Women talk in order to problem-solve and make sense of life."

By contrast, there's some evidence that men learn more effectively when they're moving around. (This may explain their predilection for doing business on the golf course.) So a woman who has a thorny issue to discuss with her male partner might consider broaching it while the two of them are on a walk.

Dr. Sax shared another interesting finding: that most women learn better at a room temperature of about 75 degrees, and men learn better at about 69 degrees. We are not sure how to explain this. Did cavewomen learn from each other around the fire, while cavemen on the hunt processed perceptions out on the chillier savanna?

Different Styles of Decision-Making

Men tend to make financial decisions in one of two ways. The first involves finding out about available choices and parsing the pros and cons of each in a rational, "thinking type" process. The second and totally opposite method, most often seen in male investors, is to act impulsively on a tip from a friend, a broker, or a TV guru. We surmise that this second mode stems from men's innate competitiveness, reflecting their desire to be one-up on other investors.

Women tend to make financial decisions slowly, often because they want more education and validation. By the same token, they are usually slower to undo a choice. Their tendency to be "buy and hold" investors has given them an edge in the past, compared with men who tend to buy and sell more frequently—often at the wrong time and at the cost of extra trading fees.

UNILATERAL VS. SHARED DECISION-MAKING

Many couples have difficulty sharing decision-making power, even when both partners earn comparable incomes. A woman often enjoys consulting her mate about even small purchases, since it reinforces her sense of togetherness, of being a team. But men often tend to make decisions, even about big purchases, without consulting their partner.

Does the following exchange sound familiar?

HE: Look what I bought us, honey! It was last year's model, so I got a really good deal on it. Isn't it beautiful?

SHE: You spent all that money without consulting me? I thought we were a team!

HE (perplexed and a little angry): I didn't know I had to ask for your permission, *Mom*.

SHE (angry and hurt): I'm not trying to be your mother! Damn it, I'm your partner!

In a guy's characteristic outlook, he's either one-up or one-down. His only experience of having to consult someone else on a decision may well have been when he asked his mother to let him buy a Star Wars action figure at Toys "R" Us. Now, if his partner suggests that they make all decisions together, he may feel attacked or demeaned.

For her part, a woman may feel hurt, angry, or betrayed by such "thoughtlessness" if she takes his tendency toward unilateral decision-making personally, rather than as an expression of his different experience of boundaries. It's another example of the difference between men's competitive view of the world and women's orientation toward cooperation and collaboration.

These attitudes are so ingrained that it is difficult to reverse them. But if men and women begin to understand each other's "culture" and learn not to take their differences personally, they may be able to negotiate agreement in structured moneytalks and goal-setting sessions, as we will see.

As a rule of thumb, men and women need to share financial decision-making and power regardless of who earns more money. In truly intimate marriages, the couple may make all decisions together, honoring her need for sharing and joint decision-making. If one or both partners want more freedom, they might agree for each to spend his or her own money without consulting the other, or for each to make spending decisions alone up to a certain dollar amount. In any case, since shared decision-making doesn't come naturally to most men, their partner may need to teach them how to do it. This will lead to a closer relationship, with the woman feeling much less hidden resentment.

Differences in Exercising Financial Power

An old jump-rope chant goes "Clap hands, clap hands till Daddy gets home. Daddy has money, and Mommy has none!" But after the post-Pill revolution sent millions of women into the workplace, and the lengthy recession starting in 2007 drove even more wives to work, there's a good chance Mommy's been bringing home a paycheck, too—possibly an even bigger one than Dad gets. Nearly 38 percent of wives earned more than their husbands in 2009, according to the most recent data from the U.S. Bureau of Labor Statistics. More than half of wives with business-related degrees outearn their husbands, reported Bernie Clark, head of Schwab Advisor Services, in a 2012 interview.[9] Working wives now contribute 47 percent of family income, on average.[10]

For many years, it was traditional for the man of the family to be in charge of investing and major spending decisions and for the stay-at-home wife to take care of everyday shopping and bill-paying. As women's social and economic stature has increased, there is much more overlap and sharing of these roles—and rightly so.

Nonetheless, many women gladly surrender financial control to their male partner. Or he may just assume this power, and she must accept her subordinate role. (For a while, anyway; many women resent the feeling of powerlessness that this engenders.) Not unexpectedly, male dominance is likelier to occur when he outearns her.

You might suppose that women who earn more than their mate would take charge of the couple's finances, but research tells us otherwise. Generally speaking, men are more comfortable than women with having primary control over the money.[11] In gay male couples, the person who earns more tends to control the money. But in gay women relationships, decisions are likely to be made jointly, no matter who earns more.

When you look at conflicts with your partner over money, see if there's a major power imbalance in your relationship. If either one of you feels uncomfortable about this imbalance, try to move toward a more equitable sharing of power. (In the next chapters, we'll explain how to tackle this difficult issue respectfully and safely.)

Sharing Power Leads to Intimacy

Differences in How the Money Is Held

Should a couple keep their money in joint accounts or separately? There's really no "should" about it, since this is something you both need to agree on. But surprisingly, men and women tend to change places in terms of who wants boundaries and who doesn't.

In Olivia's experience, the "money merger" is frequently the man, and the "money separatist" may well be the woman. Quite often, neither partner understands the other's desire. Men who want to combine the money will say, "Why do you want money of your own? Don't you trust me?" or even "Are you planning to leave me?" Women who want their own accounts will find themselves snapping, "Why do you want to merge our money? You act like you want to control me!"

There are grains of truth in each of these reactions. As the primary provider, men have traditionally been the controlling partner in a relationship. And as the lower earner or non-earner in many couples, women know they could be left financially up the creek in a divorce.[12] Even in happy marriages, women often suffer from abandonment fears or old wounds from previous relationships that make them seek the security of their own money. Though these are valid external reasons, we believe deeper longings are at work here.

Early in a relationship, many men tend to pull back at the first mention of commitment. For them, the main challenge of intimacy is learning to connect and stay connected. Thus, a man's willingness to merge his money with his partner's may be a loving expression of his desire for a more complete connection.

Women have much less trouble connecting. In fact, it's easy for a woman to "overmerge"—to lose herself in an intimate relationship—so her primary challenge is learning to preserve a sense of autonomy. Her desire for some money of her own reflects this need for healthy separateness, and may well enable her to connect with her man from a deeper, more secure place.

Of course, some couples do not fit this pattern. Both partners may be equally in favor of keeping their money separate, or of merging everything. But even couples who say they are happy merging everything may find that if the woman inherits money later on, she will prefer to keep it in her own name. This can lead to hurt feelings in her partner, who thinks, *All these years I've shared every penny with you, and now that you have some money of your own, you won't share it with me!* When there is tension around this issue, understanding both men's and women's deeper needs—his for merging and hers for some autonomy—can help resolve the problem once and for all.

Olivia's advice to couples contemplating marriage is to start by making a list of expected monthly household expenses. To cover these expenses, each partner should contribute to a joint account proportionately to his or her income. For example, if he earns twice as much as she does, he should kick in twice as much. What's left of each person's income should be held separately by the one who earned it.

Different Investment Styles and Attitudes Toward Risk

Gender differences also influence attitudes toward investing, according to Paul Greenberg, Ph.D., a psychology professor at San Diego's Brandman University. "We can see gender differences in the number of trades and risk aversion," he told us. "Men can be more motivated by euphoria-driven behavior."

Men tend to regard investing as an activity with its own potential rewards of index-beating gains (perhaps comedian Rob Becker would call this "killing the market"). To them, success is often defined in terms of beating a benchmark or their friends. As Kathleen Kingsbury puts it, winning "makes their brains happy."

To women, investment success isn't about winning or losing, but about meeting their life goals and objectives—in other words, surviving and thriving. In general, they are more concerned with being able to maintain their family's well-being from day to day. To them, investing is about having enough for what they want to do, not "winning" or beating the market.[13]

This difference has a major impact on the two genders' level of comfort with the investment process. "The whole language of investing is hostile to women," observes Eleanor Blayney. "It's no accident that the format of CNBC looks exactly like ESPN, with streaming scores. It's all about winning and losing. A man says, 'Okay, I made three percent this quarter. Is that more or less than the market? And is it more or less than the other guys?'"

"We need to look at how we define success," agrees planner Jetton, who is another founding partner of Direction$. "As Eleanor says, when you have an investment performance conversation with a man, he wants to know how his return compares to the S&P 500 and other benchmarks. Women want to know, 'What does this mean? Can I redo the kitchen? Can I retire?'"

Nowhere is the difference more plain than in investors' attitudes toward risk. Men are typically more willing to take greater risks with their money than women are. Why so? Women's long history of earning less than men, combined with "bag lady" insecurities, makes them reluctant to entrust their savings to the fluctuations of the stock market. Men's greater self-confidence and competitiveness no doubt contribute to their greater readiness to take more chances with their money.

To some extent, risk appetite versus risk aversion is in our wiring. Boys tend to exhibit riskier behavior when other boys are watching. Girls are less likely to be impressed by risk-taking behavior in their girlfriends, or to enjoy risk-taking for its own sake. Why? Blame differences in the autonomic nervous system. In boys, risky activities typically trigger a rush that they find intensely pleasurable (think paintball games, demolition derbies, extreme sports). Psychologist Dr. Sax mentions a study where youthful participants played a video game in which they risked a realistic-looking crash. Most of the boys felt exhilarated by the danger, while most girls said it made them feel fearful. In a related finding, girls tend to underestimate their chances of success in physically risky activities, and boys tend to overestimate theirs.

In fact, playing it safe could be one reason for the notorious income differential between men and women. When economist Linda Babcock studied new Carnegie Mellon University graduates, she noted that in job interviews the women didn't ask for more money, but the men did. As a result of this "risk-taking" behavior, the men were rewarded with higher starting salaries.

The most significant thing to understand about this gender difference is that for Risk Takers (who tend to be men), the act of risk-taking is experienced as intense pleasure, excitement, and freedom. When a Risk Taker avoids risks, it feels constraining and even claustrophobic. For Risk Avoiders (commonly women), conservative investments and other relatively safe financial choices feel like security and freedom. Taking risks with money feels dangerous—if not downright suicidal—to a Risk Avoider.

If you and your partner are on different ends of the risk spectrum, don't despair. It will take a great deal of openness and a willingness to experiment with each other's outlook, but if you learn to understand and move toward each other's perspective, the rewards of such non-habitual behavior will be great.

Different Styles of Philanthropic Giving

Giving to charity is another area where couples often clash. Generally speaking, men act on their competitive instincts and women follow their cooperative nature. In a *Lilith* magazine article[14] some years ago about the different philanthropic styles of Jewish men and women, it was noted that men are often motivated to donate to a cause because their colleagues are giving to it, and that the size of their contribution is a way of demonstrating clout and power. They may write a big check all at once, without asking a lot of questions about how their donation will be used. Although they are typically giving to a cause they favor, they like seeing their name atop a list as the largest donor. Another competition won!

Women tend not only to be more private in their giving but also to gather more information about the causes and charities they support. They want to know their money will be used for something they believe in. (Adam Kanzer, director of stockholder advocacy for the Domini Funds, has told us there are more women investors than men in Domini's socially responsible mutual funds. This fuels our belief that women care about feeling emotionally connected to their investments as well as to their giving.) In general, women are less concerned about how much their friends are donating, unless it is to give the same amount and thus feel more connected to them in a cooperative effort. A wealthy woman may sometimes make a larger donation in her own name, but her goal is more likely to be recognized than to one-up her peers.

There's another interesting, but not surprising, difference between the genders in philanthropy. As financial planner Blayney told us, women need to know that they have enough money before they give any of it away. "Women are far more likely to make a testamentary gift [through their will] than a lifetime gift," she said. "They're afraid to give until they're sure they have enough for themselves—even women who have plenty. [...] Until [a woman] knows what she's got, how long it's going to last, and what she needs, she can't be generous."

If you and your partner are trying to decide where and how to support charities you favor, it's important to accept each other's philanthropic style without judgment. By practicing empathy and openness, you may well be able to harmonize your differences and meet in the middle.

Different Burdens Around Money and Work

He was a rich and successful doctor, whose wife loved to entertain in their beautiful house while the kids had swim parties in the

60-foot pool or watched movies in the home theater. Anyone would suppose him to be very happy and content with his life. But as he was giving Sherry a lift to a family get-together one evening, he surprised her by confessing, "You have no idea how draining it is to work fifteen hours a day so that my wife and kids can live a life of leisure." The bitterness and sadness in his voice jarred her into the realization that despite his wealth and professional success, this man carried a burden of stress and unfulfilled needs.

Olivia has heard the same lament from male clients in her therapy practice. The fact is that despite the social changes of the past few decades, many men still feel responsible for their family's economic well-being. Even if a man earns less than his spouse, he may still feel the provider burden. A great deal of anecdotal evidence testifies to the shame and depression assailing men who could not replace a job lost in the recession and were forced to depend on their wife's earnings.

Women, on the other hand, feel the burden of the "second shift." In addition to holding down a job outside the home, they usually bear most of the responsibility for child care, housekeeping, and maintaining family relationships and social connections. Many women exhaust themselves trying to juggle all these roles week after week. According to a recent survey from the American Psychological Association, working women report higher levels of work stress than men, along with a sense of being underappreciated and underpaid.[15] If they resist learning financial management skills, the reason may simply be that they lack the energy to take on yet another job.

It hasn't always been this way. In pre–birth control pill days, teaching and nursing were the two careers open to women, who were not expected to work once they married and the children came along. The Pill initially broadened wives' choices: no longer forced to care for kids, they could stay home and write poetry, garden, or do volunteer work while Hubby continued to bring home the bacon. Part-time work allowed some wives to earn pin money. If they did elect to work full-time, they could often choose an enjoyable job regardless of what it paid. Many men, brought up to shoulder their provider burden without complaint, understandably envied this freedom. Some surely resented it.

Today it typically takes two paychecks to live as comfortably as our parents or grandparents did on one, which means that most women's options have narrowed again. Unless they are wealthy, they need to go to work. But now, being increasingly well educated and self-confident, many have a wide choice of career paths. And if and when children come into the picture, both husband and wife feel free to discuss the role they want to play. Many a husband chooses to stay home with the kids so his wife can pursue a satisfying and well-paying career.

We are still far from gender equality, of course, and most men and women still carry the traditional burdens of their sex. When you and your partner talk, empathize with each other's burden instead of arguing over which of you is working harder or suffering more. Men deserve sympathy and appreciation for carrying the heavy psychic responsibility of providers. Women need empathy and appreciation for a "second shift" burden that may include work, home, children, and elderly parents. By taking time to acknowledge the load that each of you carries, you'll help bring more harmony to your life together.

Different Fears About Money and Work

Bag lady nightmares are no respecter of wealth. Even well-off women tend to fear losing all their money and ending up on the street. Women who have inherited wealth often worry that just as their money magically appeared, so might it magically disappear.

This deep-rooted fear may go back to caveman days when a woman couldn't survive for long on her own. Today, she may worry that a lost job, a market crash, divorce, or the death of her spouse could rob her of money that she will never be able to replace.

Men tend to be more confident about their ability to support themselves financially, no matter what. (Even if they're not truly confident, they still tend to act that way.) Their deepest fears arise from their provider burden: they worry about being injured and unable to work, dying young and leaving their family destitute, or (especially in recent years of high unemployment) losing their job and being unable to find a comparable one.

As we suggested in discussing the different burdens of women and men, it's important to understand and empathize with your partner's deep fears. Mutual support and reassurance will help both of you feel less anxious about these potential traumas.

An Important Note for LGBT Couples

For same-sex couples, some of these differences may apply and others won't. Remember, it can be dangerous to embrace gender-related generalizations that aren't really applicable. As we said earlier, if the shoe doesn't fit, don't try to wear it!

Cultivating Compassion and Respect Around Differences

Near the beginning of Olivia's therapy career, she and Warren Farrell co-facilitated a workshop called "Consciousness-Raising for Men and Women." As part of this workshop, participants had to go on a "role-reversal" date with someone of the opposite sex while embodying behavioral stereotypes of the other gender. For example, women were supposed to make remarks about their date's body, open doors, and pay for the meal, and men were expected to act compliant, stroke their partner's ego with compliments, and be sexually flirty.

Sound outdated? We wish! In some cases, ingrained attitudes haven't kept up with other kinds of egalitarian progress.

This exercise helped many participants develop more empathy for the constraints that trap women and men in roles not of their own choosing. Its central idea of "practicing the nonhabitual" remains at the core of Olivia's philosophy about how people can grow and change.

Your Sixth Money Harmony Assignment

Based on what you've learned in this chapter, try to identify a gender-related difference in the attitude or behavior of someone you know of the opposite sex. Maybe the difference is in how your partner approaches solving a problem. Or how a coworker responds to being rebuffed when asking for a well-deserved raise. Or whether a sibling's reaction to news of an ailing relative is instant advice, or careful listening and sympathy. Notice how this attitude or behavior differs from your own, and see if you can adopt it for a few days or a week. Write down how it feels to be different, and reward yourself for your courage in trying on this new way of being.

If acting out the nonhabitual feels too uncomfortable, consider this instead: sitting down with that person in a relaxed place and time, discuss your new awareness of the gender difference you've noticed, and compassionately explain how it has made you more understanding of their worldview or inner landscape.

What You Can Learn from Walking in the Other Gender's Shoes

By understanding and accepting male-female differences around money with curiosity and compassion instead of defensiveness or criticism, you and your partner can create a climate of mutual respect and interest. In this forgiving environment, you will be able to figure out how to make financial decisions together and how to talk about your money in a way that minimizes conflict, tension, and misunderstanding.

7.
POLARIZATION PATTERNS: RESOLVING POWER STRUGGLES AND MOVING TOWARD THE MIDDLE

When you look around at your friends who are in couple relationships (and maybe when you reflect on your own partner, if you're in a relationship), it may seem self-evident that opposites attract. Introverts choose extroverts, footloose and fancy-free types select super-responsible types, verbal types pick nonverbal types, and people who like to cocoon often choose partners who would rather party. When it comes to money, tightwads marry spendthrifts, Worriers marry Avoiders, Planners marry Dreamers, and so on. In most cases, this polarizing dance seems inevitable.

Even when partners don't start out as opposites, they usually end up that way. (Olivia has been giving workshops on this rule of thumb for so long that one participant named it "Mellan's Law.") When two Spenders marry, for example, they will vie with each other for the super-Spender role, and the loser will become a relative Hoarder.

But over time, polarizations can become more rigid and conflict-ridden. Each partner begins to attack the other for his or her different habits. The Spender who once admired his Hoarder mate's budgeting and planning skills now accuses her of stinginess and obsession with detail. The Hoarder who used to see her partner's free-and-easy spending as spontaneous and generous now perceives it as irresponsible, immature, and selfish.

In this chapter, we will look at the most common polarizations of money personality styles and determine what can be done to harmonize these differences. In Olivia's years of doing money therapy work, she has identified these major polarizations:

Hoarder vs. Spender
Planner vs. Dreamer
Worrier vs. Avoider
Money Monk vs. Amasser
Money Merger vs. Money Separatist
Risk Taker vs. Risk Avoider

Another common polarization pattern that may affect a couple's moneylife together could be defined simply as Different Priorities. Many of us are also prone (sometimes only in small ways) to polarization around power.

We will spend some time exploring each of these polarizing dances. As you read about them, try to identify which pattern(s) you exemplify in your relationship with your partner. You may discover that you are one money type in this relationship, another type with your children, and a third type with your parents or with the boss at work. Once you've identified your major polarizations, we will give you the tools you need to begin restoring harmony in your relationships.

Hoarders and Spenders Use Money in Opposite Ways

Hoarder vs. Spender

As we know, Hoarders enjoy saving money and have a hard time spending it on anyone, including themselves. They are adept at setting budget priorities and deferring gratification. Spenders, on the other hand, enjoy spending money to bring pleasure to themselves and others. They tend to be more spontaneously generous. If they are extreme Spenders, their impulsiveness may lead to spending that is somewhat out of control.

The old stereotype is that Hoarder men are married to Spender women. (Comics have had a field day with this one!) But even if this stereotype once had some truth to it, it certainly doesn't any more. In our experience, these types are not gender-linked.

And as we mentioned, even if two partners don't start out as opposites, they will probably polarize over time. So if two Hoarders join forces, they will fight each other for the super-Hoarder role, and the loser will learn to be a comparative Spender. It's extremely rare to see a couple who are both happy Hoarders, or happy Spenders, with no polarizing tensions at all. Not impossible—but rare!

A HOARDER-SPENDER MARRIAGE: DAN AND SONDRA

Dan and Sondra, former high school sweethearts, had been married for 15 years. Growing up, Dan had been told over and over about his grandfather, who had been wealthy but lost everything in the Depression. Now a well-paid corporate executive, Dan held on to his money for dear life, afraid of losing it as his grandfather had. Sondra, who came from a working-class family, had given up her job as a teacher to stay home and raise their two children.

For Dan, money equaled security. For Sondra, money equaled love. So whenever he saved money, he felt happy and she felt deprived. Whenever she spent money, she felt happy and he felt anxious and fearful.

When they entered therapy, he griped that her shopaholic tendencies would send them to the poorhouse. Sondra complained tearfully, "He's a cheapskate! He won't even buy our kids the clothes they need to fit in at school." She went on with smoldering resentment: "All he cares about is money. For our fifteenth anniversary, all he bought me was a crummy CD. Can you imagine?"

Dan was stupefied. "I took hours off from work for three days in a row to look for that CD," he protested. "It was the song we danced to at our senior prom when I asked her to go steady. I wanted her to have a real recording, not just an MP3 download. And all she can say is that it didn't cost enough!"

Only by beginning to understand each other's world and trying on aspects of each other's money style could these two hurting, warring partners begin to harmonize their differences. Dan looked at the limitations of his excessive hoarding, and Sondra recognized the rebellious aspects of her spending. Dan could finally admit that he admired Sondra's ability to give herself and her loved ones gifts and to enjoy life in the moment. And Sondra could acknowledge that she admired Dan's ability to set spending priorities for the sake of their future security. During the course of therapy, they also learned to conduct respectful moneytalks, even about difficult subjects. (In chapters 9 and 10, you'll learn more about these structured moneytalks.)

When Dan and Sondra admitted out loud what each of them secretly admired about the other's tendency to spend or hoard, they were taking an important step toward depolarization: *acknowledging envies and appreciations of your partner's money style.*

Why don't couples do this more? Generally, at least part of the answer is fear. Dan feared that by admitting to Sondra that he admired her generosity, he would make her feel she had license to spend more freely. Sondra feared that if she told Dan she admired his ability to postpone spending and delay gratification, it would give him permission to rein her in more tightly.

Once they stopped attacking each other for their faults and complimented each other for their strengths, something unexpected happened. Sondra felt safe enough to admit that she'd like to learn more self-discipline, as Dan had, and Dan was free to admit that he'd like to relax his obsession with saving money and enjoy life more with Sondra and the kids. When a couple is locked into a polarization pattern, ending the blaming attacks and giving each other the benefit of the doubt can work wonders.

Dreamers Fantasize About Goals; Planners Make Road Maps

Planner vs. Dreamer

Planners dislike making spontaneous or impulsive decisions about money. On the contrary, they love to ponder anticipated purchases and other financial expenditures. Quite often, they are also Hoarders who enjoy setting financial priorities and saving money. They tend to be practical and objective. Dreamers are future-oriented, passionate people who enjoy fantasizing about grand schemes and all the ways they can express their creativity and full potential in their moneylife. They generally dislike planning things in minute detail, or at least they find it very difficult to contemplate future activities.

A PLANNER-DREAMER COUPLE: KATE AND MARK

Mark, a Dreamer in his 40s, wanted to quit his $120,000 a year corporate job and begin teaching emotionally disturbed kids in a special school he'd heard about. Kate, the detail person in the family, was about to write her final thesis for a graduate degree. She had looked forward to starting a career now that their daughter Emily was in college.

Kate panicked at the thought that Mark might be frustrated enough to quit his job and take a $25,000 probationary teaching contract at that special school. She envisioned catastrophic outcomes: their money wouldn't last; they would have to sell their house; Emily would have to drop out of school; she herself would have to take the first job that came along instead of one in her field of study, and so on.

When Mark and Kate came in for money therapy, Olivia and her then-partner gave them a simple assignment representing another step in the depolarization process: *learning to move toward the middle.* Every week for three weeks, Mark had to act like a Planner, writing detailed plans about how to complete his job transition without throwing the family into financial crisis. Kate had to take on the role of a Dreamer, fantasizing about all the things she yearned to do in her life and writing them down. They were also to record their feelings about these new behaviors.

Within a week or two, Mark and Kate reported having the most intimate and fruitful conversations of their long married life. Moreover, they found a creative solution to their dilemma: writing down their yearnings revealed a shared dream to travel or live abroad. They agreed that Mark would ask for a two-year transfer to his company's branch office in

Belgium. While Kate completed her graduate thesis there, Mark took summer courses in special education to "try out" this possible new field. By the time they returned to the U.S., Kate had her advanced degree and could begin earning a good salary, their daughter was almost out of college, and Mark had decided to pursue his new career path.

At that point, they both felt happy and excited about the course of their lives. Because each of them had moved toward the middle in their simple assignments, they could make decisions as a couple that satisfied them both. In just three once-a-week therapy sessions, they had completed the depolarization process.

Avoiders and Worriers Drive Each Other Crazy

Worrier vs. Avoider

Worriers tend to spend hours reviewing their bank balances online, anticipating disaster if the stock market is down for the day, and repeatedly pulling their credit reports to check for identity theft. Their money anxiety may actually verge on obsession. Avoiders, by contrast, try not to focus on their moneylife any more than they absolutely have to. They avoid reconciling their checkbook, paying bills, doing taxes, budgeting, and planning for the future.

Worriers need to step back from their excessive fears and concerns about their money. Avoiders need to face the realities of their moneylife, so they won't feel so overwhelmed on the inevitable day that they will have to start making financial decisions.

A WORRIER-AVOIDER MARRIAGE: BARBARA AND GORDON

Barbara and Gordon had been together for only two years when they came in for therapy. Barbara's first marriage had been brief and childless. She and her ex-husband had earned about the same income and had kept their money separate. Gordon was still paying alimony and child support to his first wife, to whom he had been married for 20 years. His twin sons had just graduated from college, and his youngest was starting at a prestigious Ivy League school.

A doctor with a small practice, Gordon made a substantial income. But he was a chronic Avoider. He failed to bill insurance companies on time, neglected to collect payment from patients, and paid taxes late every year. All of his disposable income went to meet his obligations to his ex-wife and family, including paying college costs for his youngest son.

Barbara admitted she was something of a Worrier, though she had never been as anxious about money as she had become since marrying Gordon. She complained that he was making no financial investment in their new marriage to show his love and support for her. However, he expected her to be loving and supportive toward his kids, and to suppress any wants or needs of her own until his last son was through with college.

In Worrier-Avoider marriages such as Barbara and Gordon's, polarization can become severe if one person enters the marriage as an extreme type. If a confirmed Worrier marries, his or her mate will become an Avoider. (Being around that much worry and tension would be guaranteed to make anyone flee from the topic of money.) On the other hand, if a dedicated Avoider enters a relationship, the other partner will become more of a Worrier, since someone has to be concerned about the realities of their financial life.

In this case, Gordon's extreme avoidance of financial matters and his tendency to overspend on his first family intensified Barbara's previously mild anxiety about money. Since their marriage, she had become a full-fledged Worrier and a more extreme Hoarder than ever before.

During therapy, both spouses wrote money dialogues and practiced nonhabitual behaviors. Gordon agreed to take on tasks he usually avoided, such as billing insurers and collecting from them; Barbara practiced short intense periods of "conscious worrying"—writing down her worries and consciously reflecting on them—so she could learn to give it up more and more.

After three months their communication had improved, and so had their relationship around money. Gordon could acknowledge how supportive Barbara was being by living frugally and paying for their needs with her own money while his youngest son was in college. Barbara could acknowledge that Gordon's responsible behavior toward his three sons reflected a loyalty that extended to her as his new wife. His loving gesture of writing her cards to express his gratitude for her helped her feel more appreciated, and his progress in collecting fees and keeping records up to date gave her a stronger sense of security.

If you and your partner are stuck in Avoider-Worrier dynamics, don't panic. With some effort and goodwill, time, and patience, you can start bringing harmony to this very common polarizing dance.

Money Monks and Amassers Live in Different Worlds

Money Monk vs. Amasser

Money Monks believe that money has the power to corrupt their values and sense of personal integrity. They prefer being on the "have-not" end of the spectrum rather than becoming an evil "have." "Poverty consciousness" (i.e., living frugally and being supersensitive to the misfortunes of others) is seen as virtuous, and amassing wealth is perceived as greedy and selfish. Money Monks often feel anxious and guilty if too much money comes to them, whether through salary increases, inheritance, or their spouse's winning the lottery.

Amassers, on the other hand, believe that money equals power and/or self-worth, but in a positive sense. It seems to them that the more money they have, the better their life will be and the better they'll feel about themselves. You can see how a relationship between an Amasser (who thinks nothing could be finer than to have lots of money) and a Money Monk (who thinks money is bad or dirty) will be fraught with tension and misunderstanding of each other's universe.

A MONEY MONK–AMASSER MARRIAGE: DEVON AND KAREN

Devon and Karen, both in their early 30s, had been married for five years. They first met while marching in a civil rights demonstration. Devon now worked for an environmental group and earned $28,000 a year. Karen, who had finished law school just before they met, worked for a small law firm that specialized in affirmative-action cases and women's issues. She made $60,000 a year and was due for a large raise in the next few months. There were other differences, too: Devon came from a working-class Catholic family of eight children; Karen was from an upper-middle-class family and had two older brothers, a doctor and an electrical engineer.

Currently, the tension in Devon and Karen's marriage centered on buying a car and taking a vacation. Devon, a Money Monk, was determined to live a life of simplicity and never become one of the "fat cats" he loathed. He was proud to drive a rusty old Volkswagen Beetle that was falling apart. Though Karen was a politically liberal activist, she liked the fact that she was making more and more money every year. She wanted to use some of her raise to take a Caribbean vacation and make the down payment on a new Honda sedan. Devon considered these desires of hers "disgustingly bourgeois."

The challenge for Money Monks and Amassers (and for any other pair of opposites, for that matter) is to change places and perspectives, at least to some degree. Even though this reversal of roles and perspectives is only temporary, it can go a long way toward building empathy for your partner's position and loosening biases and rigidities in your own moneylife.

So how did this couple resolve their differences? Both Devon and Karen searched for examples that ran counter to their own prejudices (or perhaps we should say biases). Devon was able to relax his disdain for wealth by discovering well-to-do people whom he considered to be doing wonderful things with their money. He even found examples of folks who were having some fun with their money as well as bettering the world with it. Karen located examples of people without a lot of money who were living happy and full lives. Both Devon and Karen gained insight into their own emotional baggage around money and learned to communicate with each other about it. (You'll read about their structured moneytalk in chapter 9.) Thus, each of them began to have more empathy with the other's feelings and desires.

Devon slowly learned to tolerate Karen giving herself some pleasures of life, without disrespecting her for these choices. And Karen could let Devon preserve a style of living that was more spartan than the one she would have chosen for herself. Clinical researchers Howard J. Markman and Clifford Notarius, who have spent years examining happily married versus distressed couples, report that it is not the degree of difference between members of a couple that determines their level of marital contentment, but how they handle these differences.[16] By practicing how to communicate more effectively and empathetically about their dissimilarities, Devon and Karen learned to accept them and work with them more creatively.

Money Mergers and Separatists Experience Intimacy Differently

Money Merger vs. Money Separatist

In couple relationships, Money Mergers want to merge both partners' money; Money Separatists want to keep some or all of it in separate accounts. Sometimes, of course, both partners are Mergers, or both are Separatists. Money is either merged or kept separate, and there is no tension.

But in cases where one partner is a Merger and the other is a Separatist, hurt feelings and misunderstandings can easily arise. In working with couples over the years, Olivia has found that it's often women who want at least some separate money, and men who want to merge it. If the couple get locked into negativity around this difference with each partner accusing the other of base motivations, they will both end up feeling hurt and angry. By developing an understanding of each other's deeper intimacy needs, they can work in harmony toward a mutually satisfying solution—perhaps merging some money and keeping some separate. (For more details on this topic, turn back to the discussion in chapter 6.)

A MERGER-SEPARATIST CONFLICT: ANDREW AND JULIA

On a television show where Olivia talked about couples conflicts over money, a young man named Andrew stood up to ask a question. "I'm engaged to be married, and I'm already having trouble with my fiancée about money," he said, his eyes blazing with frustration. "I talk about 'our' money, but she talks about 'her' money! That's totally unfair. What's all this about 'her money,' anyway?"

Maybe it does seem unfair—but remember, men and women have different challenges in learning to be intimate. For men, what's difficult is learning to get connected and stay connected. A desire to merge the money often reflects a man's longing for more togetherness and connection. It's one area of his life where he's capable of merging, and to many men that feels good. For women, on the other hand, connection tends to come naturally. What's hard is learning not to lose themselves in the relationship. So a woman's desire for money of her own usually reflects her longing for healthy autonomy in the midst of intimacy.

As Andrew took this all in, his anger turned to understanding and empathy. "What you're saying makes sense," he agreed. "Now maybe we can work out what to do with our money—and hers!"

Of course, it would be fine if he wanted some separate money, too. But solutions don't have to look symmetrical to work well. A couple just need to respect each other's deeper psychological needs for both healthy independence and healthy interdependence.

DEALING WITH AN INCOME DISPARITY: GLORIA AND ERIC

Whenever there's a great difference in the amount of money each person brings to a couple relationship, it's important for both partners to discuss openly how they feel about the disparity. They should also talk about who pays for what, and whether their money will be merged or kept separate.

Because of their traditional role as chief provider, men sometimes believe that they should take care of the (merged) family money. Some couples aren't bothered at all if the wife earns more than the husband. In other cases, one or both partners feel uncomfortable about it.

A woman we'll call Gloria had definite feelings on the subject. She didn't like to be constantly reminded that she made twice as much as her husband, Eric, but she did think it was fair for her to pay more for household expenses such as rent and utilities. So both partners contribute to a household expense fund at the beginning of each month, with Gloria putting in twice as much as Eric. During the month, all household bills are paid out of that pool. Gloria says, "I put in $2,000 every month, and Eric contributes only $1,000. Now that this is our habit, I'm not constantly reminded that I pay twice as much as he does for our joint expenses. The system works perfectly, and I'm proud of us for coming up with it." (As we've mentioned, we strongly favor this approach, which would work equally well when a husband earns more than his wife.)

Risk Takers Love a Thrill; Risk Avoiders Hate It

Risk Taker vs. Risk Avoider

As we explained in chapter 4, Risk Takers (usually men) like the thrill and the adventure of taking big financial risks; they're often very aggressive investors. Risk Avoiders (usually women) are much more conservative, preferring not to take the chance of losing their money. Risk Takers tend to be Dreamers; Risk Avoiders tend to be Planners. Risk Takers are often Spenders and Risk Avoiders are often Hoarders, although this is not always the case. Some women with overspending tendencies insist on avoiding risk at all costs when they invest. The Money Merger/Money Separatist and Risk Taker/Risk Avoider polarization patterns are the only two that seem to be gender-related.

When it comes to risk, one partner's hell is often the other's heaven. Risking a substantial amount of money makes the Risk Taker feel alive and free with no boundaries; it makes the Risk Avoider feel terrified, just *because* there are no boundaries. Playing it safe with money causes the Risk Taker to feel bored, depressed, and straitjacketed but makes the Risk Avoider feel safe, secure, and free—free from anxiety and fear, that is.

A RISK TAKER–RISK AVOIDER MARRIAGE: ALAN AND EILEEN

As an investor, Alan, a corporate executive, was an extreme Risk Taker. Eileen, his wife, was extremely careful with the money she earned as the manager of a bookstore. Without saying a word to her, Alan invested $20,000 in options—and lost it all. Although he kept hoping to make the money back, eventually he had no choice but to break the news to Eileen. At first in shock, Eileen soon began to feel betrayed and angry. In a gesture of apology and reconciliation, a shamefaced Alan agreed to let her handle all their money for the next couple of years.

A year went by. They were slowly recovering from their financial loss, but Alan felt like a prisoner because he was not allowed to make any risky investments. When they sought help from Olivia, she coached them to look at their own extreme Risk Taker and Risk Avoider tendencies. Slowly, each of them began to understand what it felt like to be inside their partner's skin. And they negotiated a new agreement:

- Eileen would still manage most of their money, but Alan would have a certain amount of it to spend or invest as he saw fit.

- They would meet periodically to share what was going on with their money in an open and respectful way.
- They would invest a small proportion of their money in higher-risk investments with the potential for higher returns than Eileen's choices of the past year.
- Alan would attend several meetings of Gamblers Anonymous to see if the group support there might benefit him.

Having moved toward the middle, Alan and Eileen were on their way to healing the psychological wounds of their money crisis. If you too are truly willing to walk a mile in your partner's moccasins (or even a quarter of a mile) despite the temporary feelings of discomfort, the rewards can be tremendous in terms of creativity, flexibility, and renewed intimacy.

Polarizing Around Different Priorities

Sometimes polarization is simply a matter of two partners having different priorities about what they would like to do with their money. If so, you and your mate can often reach a compromise that gives each of you some of what you want. If you understand the longings that underlie the goals you've identified, you may find you'd be just as satisfied with a different goal that isn't in conflict with what your partner wants.

CONFLICT OVER BUYING A HOUSE: JACK AND LENA

Jack and Lena were squabbling about a house. She wanted to buy a place of their own, which to her would represent "having arrived" in some sense as well as being financially secure. Jack vehemently opposed such a major purchase. His father had spent his whole life working at a job he hated just to make payments on a mortgage that was more than he could afford. Jack had vowed never to get trapped in this way.

Their dispute at first appeared insoluble, but once they began to explore their underlying feelings, they discovered that it might be possible to accommodate each other's desires. After Jack realized that his negative feelings about owning a home were attributable to his father's trauma, he was able to start thinking about buying a small house that wouldn't preempt their other spending goals. Lena felt able to look for ways to feel financially secure and successful other than through owning a home.

The better they understood their individual motivations, the easier it was for them to come up with solutions that could work well for them. (In chapter 11, we'll discuss the most effective ways for you and your partner to fulfill your individual and mutual goals.)

Polarizing Around Power

When one partner assumes the role of a powerful victimizer and the other takes on the complementary role of a powerless victim, the polarizing struggle can become laced with hostility and even, in the extreme, with violence. If nothing is done to change the pattern of these "power plays" and "paybacks,"[17] the relationship will be warped by ongoing resentment, hostility, and punishment. The chances are good that it will end in divorce.

We would all do well to consider the ways in which we perpetuate power struggles in our own relationships, perhaps by controlling information, hoarding power, keeping secrets, or resorting to behavior motivated by old grudges, rebellion, lack of trust, or lack of openness. Only by committing to sharing power, knowledge, information, and decision-making can a couple make a marriage work. The more willing we are to look at our own role in keeping these power struggles going, the clearer we will be about how to change them.

The 5 Steps of Successful Depolarization

To sum up, depolarization is possible when you take these steps:
1. Communicating openly and honestly with your partner
2. Acknowledging secret envies and appreciations of your partner's money style
3. Learning to "move toward the middle" by practicing the behaviors and attitudes that are hardest for you
4. Monitoring and recording your emotional reactions to these new behaviors and attitudes
5. Rewarding yourself for taking positive action

When a couple has successfully depolarized, this doesn't mean that the Hoarder has become a quasi-Spender and the Spender has become a quasi-Hoarder. It does mean that the couple no longer experience chronic tension between their opposing money styles. The Hoarder has probably loosened up his or her tendency to hold on to money at all costs, and the Spender may now have the choice of saving money, prioritizing for long-term goals, and sticking to a spending plan if he or she commits to one.

Can this really work? Absolutely! Let us introduce you to Maury, a Hoarder and a Worrier married to Evelyn, a Spender and an Avoider. After many happy years together, they had worked out a way to accept each other's differences and live with each other's money styles. Maury's tone of voice exhibits a loving acceptance of what he considers to be his wife's spending quirks. He jokes, "I used to say that the way we divided up the money I made in the restaurant business was to throw the money up to the ceiling. Whatever stayed up there was mine; whatever came back down was hers!"

Though this might suggest that Maury is one of those men who complain about "the wife" spending all their hard-earned money, his light and loving tone, and the other ways he talks about Evelyn, his pride in her work and in her many talents, show that this couple has achieved a fair degree of money harmony. With all our imperfections and imbalances, if we have the proper degree of empathy and respect for our partner's strengths and weaknesses (and our own), any of us can move toward this goal.

Summarizing Your Own Polarization Patterns

Now that you're aware of many of the ways couples polarize over their differences, take some time to complete the following statements:

- Our most significant polarization is...
- Our second most significant difference is...
- Our third most significant area of struggle is...
  (This is optional. Two polarizations may be responsible for most of your money conflicts.)
- I estimate that the percentage of money conflicts we have in each of these major areas is...
  Example: 60% of our conflicts are Hoarder-Spender battles; 30% are Worrier-Avoider conflicts; 10% are fights about different priorities.
- For each polarization we manifest, I estimate that the degree of polarization, on a scale of 1 to 5, is...
  Example: If 1 is the least extreme form and 5 is the most extreme, I would say that I am a 4-Spender and my husband is a 2-Hoarder. (So my behavior is more extreme than my husband's.)

Don't share these estimates with each other yet, and don't be wedded to these numbers. They merely reflect your own perception of your differences in money style.

Your Seventh "Money Harmony" Assignment

Together with your partner, practice the following exercises to help resolve polarizations that have led to conflict between you:

- Acknowledge your secret envies and appreciations of your partner's money style. Try to be as open, honest, and vulnerable with your partner as you can.
- Admit to your partner one way you would like to be more like him or her. You can write down your response first and share it verbally afterward, or simply tell your partner directly—whatever works best for both of you.
- For each polarization, select an assignment that will "move you toward the middle" (that is, move you closer to your partner's style). It can be a new action, attitude, or behavior. Make a written list of these assignments, and tell your partner about them. Do the first assignment in the next week if possible, otherwise in the next few weeks or within a month. And allow a comfortable interval between assignments so you can feel the full impact of each one.
- Monitor your reactions to these assignments or thoughts you have about them.
- Reward yourself for performing each assignment. You might consider an individual reward as well as a couples reward if you take on these tasks together.

What are the main things you learned from doing these exercises? What did you appreciate about this work? Take a few moments to jot down or notice what the depolarization process has meant for you. It's also a good idea to acknowledge your efforts in confronting such potentially difficult and complicated issues and making progress toward resolving them.

To continue along this road, you will learn some specific techniques in the next chapter that will facilitate better, more respectful communication with your partner.

8.
COMMUNICATION TECHNIQUES: DEVELOPING A CLIMATE OF RESPECT

We all know that when members of a couple are screaming at each other, they are certainly not communicating effectively. When one partner is lecturing while the other sits in stony silence, that's not effective communication either. Nor is a conversation laced with criticism and blame.

These and many other styles of ineffective communication can upset both parties without bringing them one step closer to resolving the issues that separate them. Over and over again, it becomes clear that couples simply do not have the skills to discuss highly charged topics (or, in some cases, even less emotional ones) in a way that allows them to listen with respect and respond with empathy, to negotiate calmly and rationally, and to make practical and mutually satisfying decisions together.

In this chapter, you will learn the general guidelines and specific techniques that Olivia teaches to help clients engage in respectful, productive conversations with their mates.[18] These skills can also be applied in talking with other people in your life, but in the following chapters our focus will be on discussing money and goals with your partner. Let's begin by establishing a safe emotional climate.

Guidelines for Creating a Positive Emotional Climate

Even before you start communicating, think about what would constitute practicing the nonhabitual for you. For example, if you often begin a conversation on a thorny issue by complaining, blaming, and attacking your partner for some behavior that hurt you or made you angry, try acting in a new way by focusing on your softer, more vulnerable feelings of hurt while taking care *not* to express blame or anger. You may still feel this anger, but choose not to express it the way you used to. By the same token, if your mate's usual tendency when you explode in anger is to withdraw in silence and shut down, choosing to express his or her feelings verbally is practicing the nonhabitual. Even though you may not love having resentment or anger directed at you, it can be refreshing to get a new reaction for a change! As long as your partner's response is controlled and respectful, you should seriously consider accepting it.

Look at your own shortcomings first, instead of focusing on what your partner needs to do differently. Practice saying, "I'm sorry I did that; I'll try to do better next time"—and meaning it—instead of lapsing into defensive excuses for your behavior. If your partner is upset at you for something you've said or done, and you are sure that older wounds predating your relationship have intensified that reaction, acknowledge the part that you *did* play in upsetting him or her (whether you meant to or not). Give your mate the space to tend to these old wounds after you have helped heal the present one.

Practice looking at the positive qualities of your relationship, and of your partner. John Gray, the author of *Men Are from Mars, Women Are from Venus,* wrote that if a woman treats a man as if he were perfect, he will change in that direction over time. This works the other way around, too. What you focus on will grow. If you focus on the negative, that will dominate. Accentuating the positive will leave you with a lot more energy to deal with the negative.

Assume that win-win solutions are possible, even when the two of you disagree. If you and your partner take the time and effort to communicate your underlying needs and feelings and hear each other with empathy and compassion, in many cases you will find your different needs aren't in direct conflict.[19]

Minimize blame by using "I-messages" whenever possible. In general, talk about your own feelings instead of focusing on your partner's behavior or guessing at his or her negative motives. For example, if you're bothered by your spouse's habit of occasionally going to bed early without saying good night to you, try saying, "When you leave for bed without saying good night, I feel hurt; I feel ignored; I feel as if I don't exist; I feel rejected." Don't say, "I feel that you are an insensitive schmuck for going to bed without saying good night to me!" Even though the second remark uses the "I" form, it is *not* an "I-message." It's a thought or judgment that will be met with defensiveness and counterattack.

Practice hearing and repeating what your partner communicates to you before launching into your own emotional reactions. If you slow down the communication in this way, it will help both of you feel closer and more connected, and prevent you from getting into old, chronic patterns of attack and counterattack, or blame and defense.

If you are upset, see if your partner is willing to hear your feelings before you launch into your communication. Think about the nature of the message you will be sending, and announce it to your partner. Let's say you are feeling stirred up, hurt, or angry. You could tell your partner, "I'm feeling upset about something," instead of immediately starting a diatribe about what is upsetting you. Giving your mate this respectful warning will go a long way toward clarifying the communication. Asking if your partner is willing to listen also demonstrates that you respect his or her psychic space and that you take responsibility for your feelings.

When your partner opens up to you and shares sensitive facts or feelings, receive that sharing as a gift. Despite how tempting it might be to say things like "Now I understand why you're so weird in that way," make a commitment not to use this information against your partner in future discussions or as ammunition for later fights.

Good Communication About Money Deepens Intimacy

Exercises for Fostering a Positive Emotional Climate

The following exercises are designed to help you and your partner create a safe environment in which to tackle areas of chronic conflict. In such an environment, both partners should feel secure enough to reveal what kind of feedback they want, to listen and respond with empathy, and to share feelings—both the good and the bad. Although some of these exercises may initially strike you as contrived, give them all a try.

"MY PERFECT CONVERSATION"

If you often feel frustrated in conversations with your partner, especially about difficult or emotional topics, try "My Perfect Conversation," an exercise Olivia created for her clients. In this exercise each partner takes time, *before* giving details of their communication, to announce in general terms the subject they want to talk about and the ideal response they would like to receive.

Let's say that Nancy and Bill have decided to talk about their experiences at work, and Nancy will go first. Nancy tells Bill, "I'll talk about all the things that went wrong today, and some of the good things too. I would like you to look me in the eye as much as you can, smile at me warmly and sympathetically—or at least look friendly and accepting—and say emotionally supportive things like 'That's wonderful, honey,' or 'Oh, I'm so sorry to hear that; it must have been frustrating,' or 'I would have hated that, too.' In short, I want you to put yourself in my place and be as warm and empathetic as you can."

Then Nancy talks for five or 10 minutes, and Bill tries to do what she asked him to do. Afterward Nancy gives him positive feedback about what worked well. If Bill does it mostly "wrong" and says nothing, but still looks Nancy in the eye and acts warm and accepting, Nancy tells him that she appreciates these positive responses. Even though it might seem tempting to attack him for not saying anything, it's extremely important for both partners to stick to their commitment of offering only positive feedback.

Now the couple switch roles. Bill says, "I will talk about my day today, and I want you mainly just to listen without taking what I say and relating it to yourself, or changing the subject, or taking it anywhere else. Even listening silently is fine. I just want to be really heard and accepted fully." Then Nancy listens, and afterward Bill tells her what she did right.

We recommend that you and your partner do this exercise every day or every other day at first. It will take up only 10 or 20 minutes of your time, which even the busiest of couples should be able to manage. Eventually, you can practice it from time to time to keep current on your mutual needs and thus have more satisfying conversations.

POSITIVE WARM-UPS

If you want to maintain love and goodwill in a couple relationship, it's vital to keep giving your partner compliments, appreciations, and other positive strokes. Most of us have no trouble doing this during the honeymoon phase of a relationship, when the ratio of positive to negative comments tends to be 100 to 1. That ratio starts to decline after the relationship has gone on for some time, says Dr. Warren Farrell, who specializes in couples communication. Farrell believes couples must keep the proportion of positive to negative comments at 4 to 1 if they are to maintain a healthy, loving relationship.[20]

As many married couples know, this is easier said than done. We all have a habit of perceiving the cup as half empty instead of half full. But when you reverse this pattern and work at concentrating on the good stuff, your partner will almost miraculously feel safe and appreciated enough to want to change in a more positive direction.

There's a simple technique that can help you and your mate feel good enough about yourselves and each other to willingly work toward changing for the better: Begin communication sessions by sharing one or two "positive warm-ups" with each other. For example, any of these opening lines will help establish an atmosphere of mutual appreciation:

- Here's something you did recently that I appreciated a lot…
- One of the things I like best about you is…
- One of the first things I admired about you was…
- I love you most when you…
- I like the way you look when you…
- We make a good couple because…
- I'd like to thank your mother and father for making you…
- One of the things I've learned from you is…
- One of your strengths that I've benefited from is…
- One of the ways you complement (balance) me is…
- You make me happy when you…
- One of my fondest memories about us is…
- One of your most endearing qualities about money is…

After each of you has shared one or two warm-ups from the list, you will be in a more positive frame of mind and better able to discuss even thorny issues in your moneylife together.

THE MIRRORING EXERCISE

Listening and reflecting techniques can help free up communication among family members who have too much experience in pushing each other's buttons. It's particularly important to learn not only to listen to the message your partner is sending, but also to play back the spirit and content in a way that captures the essence of the message. An exercise that Olivia has found particularly useful is one she learned directly from Harville Hendrix, author of *Getting the Love You Want: A Guide for Couples* and a clinical pastoral counselor known for his work with couples.[21]

This "mirroring" exercise is done in pairs of a speaker and a listener. The ground rules are that the listener must empty his or her mind in order to enter the speaker's world. Only when it's his time to speak is he allowed to regain his own viewpoint.

The exercise begins with each person offering an appreciation of the other. It continues as follows:

Step 1: Mirroring. The speaker says a few sentences about whatever topic they are discussing. The listener "mirrors" this comment, playing it back as close to verbatim as possible and ending with "Is there more?" The speaker "sends" a few more sentences, which the listener plays back by saying, "You want to make sure that... [repeating whatever the speaker just said]. Is there more?" Eventually, the speaker says, "No, there's no more."

Step 2: Validation. The listener enters more deeply into the mind and heart of the speaker by tuning in, in the most compassionate, nonjudgmental way possible, to what "makes sense" from the speaker's perspective. For example, if the speaker says, "I feel anxious about giving you too much money all at once," the listener validates this with a response like "It makes sense that you feel anxious about giving me too much money all at once, because in the past, I have been an overspender." Then the listener should ask, "Is there any part of your message you'd like to hear validated that hasn't been validated yet?"

Step 3: Empathy. Once all the validations have been shared, the listener deepens her empathy about the speaker's emotions by saying, "I imagine you might also be feeling..." with an appropriate term such as *angry, sad, hopeful,* or *relieved.* (This should be just one word—*angry,* for example, not *angry because...* or *angry about....*) Then the speaker and listener switch places.

This exercise may sound laborious, but it slows down family members' habitual communication patterns: failing to listen carefully, interrupting, interjecting their own opinion, or agreeing without fully grasping the emotional impact of the other person's perspective. In this safe space, they learn to listen more deeply when others are speaking to them. If a couple does this exercise often enough, they can negotiate almost anything.

THE LOVE LETTER TECHNIQUE

Suppose you are too upset with your partner to even try to listen with compassion and understanding. You'd rather fire away with blasts of your hurt and anger. If you feel this way, it's time to learn an exercise created by John Gray.[22] This exercise involves writing a "love letter" to your partner in which you walk through a series of emotions in order to clarify and let go of whatever is blocking you from communicating openly with him or her.

To write this love letter, you'll need to go off by yourself to collect your thoughts and feelings. Imagine that your partner will read this letter with love and understanding. Begin with why you feel anger toward him or her ("I am angry because..."). Then explain why you feel sadness ("I am sad because..."), then fear, then regret, and finally love. Include all five sections in every letter, moving from the negative emotions to the more positive ones, and writing a few sentences about each. Try to keep each section about the same length, and write in simple terms. Don't stop until you have expressed your love in the final section. Sign the letter.

Note that in the anger section, you can also express feelings of hurt or frustration. In the sadness section, you can write about feeling disappointed. Include in the regret section apologies, feeling sorry, feeling embarrassed or ashamed, wishing that things had gone differently. The love section is the place for appreciations and positive wishes, or just a simple, straightforward expression of your love.

After you have written a love letter, write an ideal response that reflects exactly what you would want your partner to say if she or he read your love letter in the most accepting way. You might begin your response letter with a phrase like "Thank you for..." "I understand..." "I am sorry..." "You deserve..." "I want..." or "I love you...."

You may find it's unnecessary to share either of these letters with your partner because the process of writing them has put you in a more open and loving mood, ready to communicate about the task at hand. But if you discover that it works better for you to share these letters, that's fine too. In rarer cases, you may even feel so complete after writing the initial love letter that you dispense with the response letter, as Dan and Sondra do in chapter 10. Use this "love letter" technique in whichever way suits you best.

The Structured Communication Format

You are now ready to learn a structured communication technique adapted from Isaiah Zimmerman, a clinical psychologist who practices in Washington, D.C. Olivia has used this technique for years to help couples communicate clearly and thoroughly, even when discussing the most emotionally charged issues.

This technique may seem very formalized, but Olivia has found that it creates more safety and reduces the intensity of communication for couples who have a history of conflict or emotional explosions. (Others who do not experience so much friction may find the mirroring exercise can help them without such a complex structure.)

To ensure success, you first need to agree to abide by the following ground rules:

Set an approximate time limit for each communication. Limit your sharing to no longer than three minutes or so, to avoid long monologues or tirades.

Don't interrupt. When your partner has the floor, try to listen undefensively and with an open mind as much as possible.

Announce the nature of the message you will be sending. After choosing one of the following four channels of communication, ask, "Are you willing to listen?"

- The unequal channel. If you are feeling angry, hurt, resentful, disappointed, or one-down in any other way, say, "I'm angry," or "I'm hurt," or "I'm upset."
- The equal channel. If you want to share a neutral or positive thought or feeling, tell your partner, "I have a thought (or a feeling) I want to share."
- The verification channel. To see if you understand your partner's point of view, announce, "I want to verify what you just said."
- The negotiation channel. If you want to strive for settlement on something, say, "I have a negotiation." This is the only action channel.

In any of these cases, identifying and announcing the nature of the message will make your partner feel respected and "warned" about where you want to go in your communication. Then:

Ask whether your partner is willing to listen. Ask, "Can you truly listen with an open mind, or do you feel defensive about what you imagine I might say?" Give your partner some time to consider this. Anyone who can't answer "Yes" with an open heart should say "No."

Respect a "no" as well as a "yes." Communicate only when and if your partner is willing to listen. If the answer is "yes," your partner should say yes. He or she should have full permission to say "no"—for now.

If you say "no" to listening, take the initiative in continuing the dialogue. The one who says "no" can either ask for time to share upset or negative feelings that are blocking the listening process, or ask to return to this discussion at a specific time in the future.

If you say "yes," commit to listening undefensively and without interrupting.

Announce when you're done. Say, "I'm finished."

Verify your partner's feelings whenever possible. If your partner has shared a feeling and you are willing to verify what was said and felt, then do so. Next ask, "Did I hear you as you wished to be heard?" (Don't just say, "Did I get it right?" One of the most important reasons for playing back or verifying what you heard is to communicate the *spirit* of the message as well as its literal content.) This allows your partner to give you feedback on whether you gave an appropriate response, missed something, or misheard. Tell your partner what percentage of the message he or she reported well.

You don't always have to give feedback to your partner's verification attempt. If your partner has not verified your message very well and you find yourself angry that he or she *didn't* hear you in the right spirit, beware of lunging into a full-scale attack about how often you are unheard and misunderstood. If you need to share your anger, it's fine to announce that you have an "unequal," ask if your partner is willing to listen, and communicate your anger or disappointment at being misunderstood. Or if you feel grateful for your partner's attempt to understand, you could share a positive feeling—an "equal"—with your partner's permission, of course. Then, decide whether to share feedback on what percentage of your message he or she heard well.

Don't try to negotiate until after your feelings have been aired. Share negative feelings with your partner, and have your partner listen and verify your feelings with empathy and compassion. Difficult feelings must be aired, shared, and understood before a couple can negotiate successfully.

Negotiation is the only action channel. If you want to negotiate changes in behavior, it's polite (but not absolutely necessary) to first offer something your partner might want, and then ask for what you want. The only things that can be negotiated are actions and behaviors.

Feelings *cannot* be negotiated. So although you can ask your mate not to yell at you, you can't ask your mate not to be angry. We all have the right to feel whatever emotions have a grip on us.

Try sitting back-to-back. Sometimes one or both of you may feel safer and can open up more if you don't make eye contact while sharing difficult material. Consider sitting back-to-back while the two of you share hurt, angry, or stirred-up feelings, and turn to face each other when you exchange neutral or positive remarks.

If tempers flare, try to cool things off. Consider taking a break until you can review with a little more objectivity what got you so riled up. Another option is to sit back-to-back and ask for permission to communicate in the "upset" mode. If your partner offers a genuine "yes," you can push out your upset feelings until you really feel a sense of closure. (You'll know you've reached this point when you find yourself thinking, *Whew! What a relief! I'm glad I said this. It feels so good to get it out.*)

Communicating in a Structured Format

Now that you know the framework of this structured communication format, we recommend making an opportunity to practice it. If there's something difficult you would like to discuss with your partner, follow these steps:

1. Establish a safe climate with positive warm-ups. (See preceding section for examples.)
2. Share hurt, angry, resentful, stirred-up feelings. (Consider sitting back-to-back, at least for this part and perhaps until the last step.)
3. Listen empathetically and verify each other's feelings wherever possible before moving on to your own emotional reactions. If you can't listen with compassion, share your own upsets first, and verify later.
4. Negotiate with each other, and suggest actions and behaviors that would alter your usual patterns.

5. Share positive cool-downs, such as the following:
    - What I most appreciated about you today was...
    - When you express yourself, I value the way you...
    - Here's what I appreciated about what you said....
    - I learned to understand you better by...
    - You helped me feel understood and heard when you...

When you practice any of the techniques in this chapter, write down your thoughts and feelings about what it was like. Then reward yourself for this new behavior.

Using Some of These Techniques in Structured Moneytalks

Having learned a variety of couples communication techniques, you're now ready to begin exploring your respective histories around money in more depth. In the first structured moneytalk (chapter 9), where you'll be given the subjects to discuss and the order in which to discuss them, you'll need to use only a few aspects of the structured communication format.

You don't have to sit back-to-back, or ask for permission to communicate in prescribed channels. But we do recommend that you listen respectfully without interrupting each other, make a commitment not to use any of this shared information against your partner at a later date, start with warm-ups, and end with cool-downs. Toward the end of the session, you may also want to verify or mirror what your partner has shared. When you move on to more emotionally charged topics in a second structured moneytalk (chapter 10), you will need to observe the full set of guidelines presented in this chapter.

9.
STRUCTURED MONEYTALK I:
SHARING YOUR MONEY
HISTORY

If you're in a committed relationship, no matter how long the two of you have been together, we'll bet you don't know a lot about each other's money history. Since money is such a taboo subject in our culture, sharing our past experiences with it is not usually part of ordinary communication.

That was a major problem for Devon and Karen. Remember this couple from chapter 7? Devon cherished his simple lifestyle. He felt fine making only $28,000 a year with a nonprofit environmental organization in Washington, D.C., an expensive city to live in. His car was a rattletrap old Volkswagen Beetle, and he had great contempt for "bourgeois" folks around him who drove expensive cars and vacationed in fancy places. Karen, a lawyer for an activist firm, was an Amasser—compared with Devon, at least. She would have liked to take a nice summer vacation with him and buy herself a new Honda Accord, but her Money Monk spouse scoffed at such ideas.

As the first step in a communication process that could help restore their closeness, Devon and Karen decided to have a moneytalk to share their money history. Even though they had been together for more than five years and shared a lot in other areas, Karen observed (and Devon agreed) that when it came to money, they really didn't know much about each other's past.

In this chapter, we will listen in on Devon and Karen's moneytalk. At the same time, you'll learn how you and your partner can have a similar conversation of your own. (Feel free to change the order proposed here if another sequence would work better for you.) If you make time for this, bearing in mind all you've just learned about respectful communication, you'll be pleasantly surprised at how much closer you feel to each other.

Starting Your Structured Moneytalk

This first structured moneytalk is for sharing information and feelings, not for exploring conflicts related to money. As you and your partner get ready for your talk, follow these suggestions:

Find an unstressful time. Set aside a time when neither of you feels hassled or stressed and your attention is not divided. This may be easier said than done in your stressful life, but don't use that as a cop-out; find a time when you're less stressed than usual. This will allow you to devote quality time to this important conversation, and ideally to listen to each other with patience and respect.

Use your most effective communication style. Do you communicate best in writing? If so, you can write your responses to the discussion points and either share them one by one during the course of the moneytalk or save them all to discuss at the end. If you are better at ad libbing on the spot, it's perfectly all right to respond orally, trusting that what emerges is what you want and need to say. Don't worry if you and your partner have different preferences. For example, you could write your responses, while your partner responds orally.

Begin with appreciations. Choose one or two warm-up messages from chapter 8 (or better still, create your own) to communicate what you appreciate about your partner or about the connection between the two of you.

Take turns communicating your appreciations. Avoid interrupting each other. The listener's task is merely to listen respectfully and with empathy.

Skip over—for the time being—anything you can't answer. But do think about it and try to come back later to share your answers with your partner.

Here's how Devon and Karen handled this first segment of their moneytalk.

DEVON AND KAREN BEGIN WITH WARM-UPS

KAREN: I appreciate the way you've been fixing me dinner the nights I have to work late at my law office. I know it's lonely for you to be alone at night so often, so I really appreciate how thoughtful you've been toward me when I get home.

DEVON: I appreciate your sense of humor in general. When I get too intense and serious about my environmental work, you have a way of helping me lighten up that makes me feel good about being with you.

As a result of sharing their positive appreciations, Devon and Karen already felt much closer and more willing to open up to each other.

Sharing Your Money History: Beginning with Your Childhood

Next, share with your partner the messages about money that you recall from your childhood. (As we discussed in chapter 2, these

can have a strong influence on your beliefs and behaviors as an adult.)
You don't need to address all the points in the following outline, just
the ones that evoke a natural response:

1. This is how my parents handled money:
   - How they spent it...
   - How they saved it...
   - How they talked about it (or didn't talk about it, or screamed about it, or worried aloud about it)...
   - How they dealt with allowances with me (and my siblings)...
2. Here are some of my specific childhood money memories:
   - Of my parents...
   - Of siblings and other relatives...
   - Of my peers...
   - Of school (with teachers or mentors of any kind)...
   - Of religious school (if this applies)...
3. From my family, I received (directly or indirectly) the money messages that...
4. From my peers, I received (directly or indirectly) the money messages that...
5. From my religious training, I received the money messages that...
6. From the culture at large (TV shows, ads, movies, etc.), I received the money messages that...
7. I reacted to these messages by making the following vows about my moneylife:
   - To be just like _____ in this way...
   - *Never* to be like _____ in this way...
   - To deal with money in this way...
   - And to...
8. In my family, I think money symbolized...
   (choices: *love, power, control, independence, dependency, self-worth, security, freedom, corruption, and/or any other responses that seem to fit*)
9. Here's how this may be affecting me today....

The two of you can jump back and forth with each of you talking about a few of these points at a time, or each of you can opt to address all of the points at once. Whichever method you choose, take care to respect your partner's capacity to handle information. Sharing too much may make a listener feel overloaded or stressed and a speaker irritable or defensive.

After you and your partner have finished communicating your early memories around money, you may want to take a break. When you're ready, you can move on to the next section, in which you will explore how the past may be influencing the present.

DEVON AND KAREN'S FIRST SHARING OF PAST HISTORY

While reading the suggested outline, Devon jotted down notes on each point, which he referred to as he told Karen about his money history.

DEVON: My dad was a bricklayer who worked day and night to make enough money to support us. My mom stayed home with us eight kids and slaved around the house, trying to keep everything under control. They never fought about money. Mom was frugal, and they both knew they didn't have a lot. We rarely went on a vacation.

How did my family spend money? Only on necessities. How did they save it? They had virtually nothing to save. How did they talk about it? They both criticized the rich, greedy people who had money but only spent it on themselves. My dad sometimes worked for those filthy rich people—that's what he called them—and he'd talk about the disgusting amount of waste he saw in their homes.

As far as allowances are concerned, none of us kids got one until we were about 15. Then I got $5 a week, and I had to pay for what I wanted out of that. We all wore hand-me-downs. Sometimes we kids fought with one another about wanting what the other had, but that seemed normal in our big family. Our big treat was going to a movie about once a month. Once my father caught my brother Lou stealing candy in a store. Dad beat him and didn't let him watch TV or leave the house for a week, except to go to school.

We went to Catholic school, where many of the kids were pretty poor, but there were others who had much more money than we did. We felt superior to the rich kids, in a strange way. We thought we were purer than they were and knew about "real life" in the "real world." We actually talked about how we would go to heaven, and the rich kids would probably go to hell!

The nuns said things like "Money is the root of all evil." I believed them completely, and I guess I still do. In some way, money symbolizes to me greed and corruption. I guess I fit the Money Monk description perfectly, don't I? [Karen could have responded with a comment like "You sure do, and it drives me nuts sometimes," but she just listened respectfully. Kudos to her!]

When I think about my childhood and the money messages I got from that time, I think I told myself not to focus on any of the material deprivation I may have felt. I told myself I would make sure money was never that important to me; and that I would never become greedy, selfish, and corrupt like those guys my dad worked for in those big brick houses.

Now it was Karen's turn to share. She had decided to talk spontaneously without writing down her answers first. But she had read the discussion points in advance and had thought about what she remembered from her childhood.

KAREN: I grew up in a fairly wealthy suburb of Chicago. We had everything we wanted, pretty much. My parents were different from each other. My mom liked to spend money on nice things for our house and clothes for her and us, and for my father, too. My dad preferred to save his money for great vacations and for the future (college for us kids and retirement). My folks argued about whether to spend or save, but the arguments weren't too terrible. Like low-level static in our home.

My brothers were older than I was and got more money for their allowances, of course. I thought that was unfair and I told my folks, but I didn't get anywhere.

Most of my friends at school had a fair amount of money, too. But there was one girl in my class, Bobbie, my good friend, who came from a much poorer family. I used to lend her lunch money a lot, and sometimes money for clothes too. My parents found out about it and told me not to do it any more. I think I felt guilty about having more money than Bobbie, but I also liked being able to help her out.

I was afraid to cross my parents so I stopped lending her money, but I was too ashamed to tell her why. This created a big rift in our relationship; for weeks she barely talked to me. I was hurt about the tension and distance I felt between us. I think I vowed that when I was older, I would try to make a lot of money and help a lot of people who didn't have as much as I did. I think that fuels my desire to make more money today—both to enjoy it myself and to give some of it away. To me, money symbolizes freedom and independence. The more I have of it, the more I can do what I really want. At least, that's what I tell myself.

Karen felt she had revealed enough about herself for now. She and Devon agreed to return to their moneytalk the next afternoon, when she could share more of her money history and listen to the next segment of Devon's.

What they had learned had already made them more sensitive to each other's feelings. Karen began mentally scaling down her vacation plans so Devon would be more comfortable going along with her. Devon's realization that his family had hardly ever taken a vacation was helping him open up to the possibility of enjoying a getaway with his wife. He also started to understand why Karen might want to buy herself a new car.

Back to You: Getting to Know You Better

If you and your partner are willing to move to the next phase of your moneytalk, share your responses to these discussion points with each other:

- Today, I think that money symbolizes…
  (*happiness, love, power, control, independence, dependency, self-worth, security, freedom, corruption, and/or other responses that seem to fit*)
- Here's how I handled money before we met...
- I am closest to the following money personality type(s)…
  (*Hoarder, Spender, Binger, Money Monk, Avoider, Worrier, Amasser, Risk Taker, Risk Avoider*)
- I would like to move toward this money type(s)...
- I would like to move away from this money type(s)...
- Here are some other ways I'd like to change my money attitudes and behaviors...
- You might be able to help me move closer to my goals by...

The last sentence is tricky to complete. It's better to avoid statements like "If you would spend less, I could spend more." Ask for help with your own issues only if you are truly willing to accept your partner's assistance. If not, you may want to skip this point and possibly return to it at a later time.

Sharing a Loving and Vulnerable Conversation

KAREN AND DEVON CONTINUE THEIR MONEYTALK

Karen and Devon decided to discuss the points in this section by switching back and forth, sharing information in smaller pieces. This time, Karen went first.

KAREN: I think money still symbolizes freedom and independence to me. It also symbolizes power somewhat: both power to have and do what you want, and power in the world, both for good and for evil.

Before we met, I used to indulge myself more: eating out in nice restaurants when I had the money—and feeling somewhat guilty about this, since some of my friends couldn't afford it. I used to buy more clothes than I needed and plan more and more elaborate vacations. I guess I am a combination Spender and Amasser, a little bit of a Worrier, with flickers of Money Monk consciousness thrown in. I'm a little afraid of being too wealthy and losing my values, but I really don't think I will. When it comes to investing, even though I haven't had much to invest, I'm a Risk Avoider.

DEVON: I still think money symbolizes greed and corruption. I pride myself on living simply. I like driving around in my old VW Bug, and I like the fact that we have only one car and ride our bikes and take public transportation a lot, even though it takes us more time to get to work. I am clearly a Money Monk and, to some extent, an Avoider. I just don't like to deal with the details of my moneylife. I'm happy to have you take care of all of that for both of us! I'm glad I make only $28,000 a year. When people tell me that that's barely enough to survive on, it makes me feel more proud and defiant.

KAREN: I'd like to worry less about money and be less obsessed with making sure I have enough to be able to do anything I want to do. I'd also like to feel fine about spending it on what makes me feel good, as long as I do it in moderation, and still give away some money to causes I want to support. I'd like to reduce the tension between us about spending on things that aren't necessities. Even if you feel judgmental sometimes, you could help me by agreeing not to *act* judgmental when I do want to spend on something pleasurable. You could also help me see that I am free to pursue my dreams and goals, even if I don't have a tremendous amount of money. You could do this by listening to me talk about my deeper longings and dreams, and brainstorming with me about how I could achieve them.

DEVON: It's hard for me to admit this, but I actually would like to trust myself more and know that more money will not make me sell out and lose my commitment to the values I hold dear. I *would* like to enjoy a vacation with you without feeling guilty; and maybe my old car *is* falling apart, and I could tolerate it if you did buy a Honda Accord and if we used it sometimes to go to work. God, I'm actually flinching while I say this, but I know rationally that what you want is not awful or ridiculous but is really okay—for you, at least. And maybe, eventually, for me.

You could help me with all this by agreeing not to act judgmental about my extreme Money Monk tendencies but to help me to stretch a little beyond them. Maybe if you showed me how to do online banking on our computer at home, I wouldn't hate keeping track of my money so much.

Preserving Safety in Your Own Structured Moneytalk

Remember to respect the fragile nature of the communication you and your partner are having. Avoid the temptation to say, "I always knew your tightness came from your skinflint father," or "Well, now that you know that about yourself, what are you gonna do about it?" It's crucial not to use any of this shared information against each other, now or in the future. If you want this process to deepen your relationship and your intimacy, you need to create a safe space in which information can be shared and heard. And developing compassion for your partner's money roots, challenges, and struggles will deepen your intimacy tremendously.

Optional Portions of the Moneytalk

SECOND MARRIAGES

If you were married before, or lived with someone else in a long-term intimate relationship, it may be useful to share the following additional information with your new partner. Remember, each of you takes a turn, with no interruptions, comments, judgments, or even questions from the listener.

- In my last significant relationship/marriage, we handled money as follows...
- We used to fight about...
- After that experience, I vowed that never again would I...
- Some of the things I learned and value from that experience are...

Avoid getting into heated discussions on any of these points. You'll be able to address more loaded issues in the second structured moneytalk (in chapter 10).

SHARING YOUR MONEY DIALOGUES

If you both wrote money dialogues (see chapter 5), you may want to share them with each other to conclude this initial moneytalk. However, if you are the only one who has done a dialogue, you may end up feeling too vulnerable if you show it to your partner. Instead of attacking your mate for not having done a dialogue, focus on the progress you made in this moneytalk and the positive sharing you accomplished. Remember: if you focus on the positive, it will grow.

MIRRORING WHAT YOUR PARTNER SHARED

The sharing process may bring up fairly loaded issues. As noted, do *not* plunge into them right now. Instead, practice the mirroring (hearing and listening) exercise described in chapter 8. This can deepen feelings of empathy and safety, helping to make your partner feel that you are genuinely trying to put yourself in his or her shoes.

Reinforcing Progress for Yourself and Your Partner

Here is the final series of discussion points for your first moneytalk:
- Here's what I appreciate about the work I've done today...
- Here's what I appreciate about the work you have done today with me...
- Some of the important things I remembered (or shared) about myself were...
- I'm glad that you told me...
- To reward ourselves for having had this moneytalk, I suggest we both...

A joint reward is preferable, but two separate rewards are all right, too. If you're feeling particularly celebratory, you could decide to treat yourselves to a joint reward as well as individual ones.

DEVON AND KAREN'S POSITIVE REINFORCEMENT SESSION

Devon and Karen had accomplished a tremendous amount in their open and honest moneytalk. Here's what they appreciated about themselves and each other:

DEVON: I appreciated that I was willing to focus on subjects related to money for such a long time—for me!—and that I took the time and made the effort to cover all the points in the outline. Also, that I was willing to admit some of my own idiosyncrasies around my Money Monk personality.

I appreciated your openness in sharing similar information about yourself. I never felt judged or attacked by you; and I *really* appreciated that. I learned about ways that your childhood was totally different from mine, and ways that you were hurt by not being able to be as generous as you wanted to be. That made me feel much closer to you. I'd like us to reward ourselves with a picnic in the park and maybe even go to a movie later. [Devon laughed at his tentativeness about spending money on something he would enjoy. He had become much more aware of his kneejerk guilt reaction to "selfish" spending on personal pleasure.]

KAREN: I appreciated my own willingness to look at my imperfections around money. I also appreciated my commitment to remain gentle and nonjudgmental with you, and to listen carefully and respectfully. It's a habit I'd like to practice more.

I appreciated your honesty with me about areas of your moneylife that you didn't feel great about. I learned a lot from hearing about your Catholic school training. What you told me about your dad and mom judging wealthy people really helps me understand you better. I think I'll be able to be more tolerant of, and gentle with, the Money Monk in you. And now I can see that the Money Monk in me needs to do a little work, too! I think your reward of a picnic in the park and a movie later is a great idea. I accept!

Don't be concerned if you feel you did not accomplish as much as Karen and Devon did in your own first structured moneytalk. At the very least, you opened up a channel of communication that will eventually lead to better sharing and deeper intimacy—especially if you keep practicing good communication skills.

We recommend setting a date for your next moneytalk, in which you will confront and resolve more emotionally loaded topics or more highly charged dynamics in your couple relationship. (We'll introduce you to this in the next chapter.) If you are not yet ready to commit to a specific date, agree to get back together within a certain period of time (in the next two weeks, for example, or before a month is out). This will help you sustain your progress.

10.
STRUCTURED MONEYTALK 2: TACKLING YOUR MONEY CONFLICTS

Now that you and your partner have spent some time talking about emotions from the past that influence your present-day relationships with money, you are ready to embark on a more risky venture: discussing areas of conflict in your moneylife together. Using the techniques of structured communication that you learned in chapter 8 and practiced in chapter 9, you should be able to navigate these deep (and sometimes choppy) waters successfully.

Since this will be one of the more difficult stages of your journey toward money harmony, we'll show you exactly how one couple conducted this type of moneytalk. We strongly recommend that you read this sample conversation carefully before attempting your own moneytalk with your partner.

The couple we'll focus on are Dan and Sondra, whom we met in chapter 7. As you may remember, Dan was a Hoarder and a Worrier; Sondra was a Spender and an Avoider. For Dan, money equaled security; for Sondra, money equaled love. They had been a couple ever since high school, and had recently had a painful fight about their fifteenth anniversary. Dan had spent hours and hours looking for "their song"—"My Prayer"—which he felt would make a thoughtful and sentimental anniversary present. When he found it, he was ecstatic. But Sondra felt hurt when she saw the gift. She had been hoping for an expensive piece of jewelry, and the CD seemed chintzy and insignificant to her.

After Sondra told him what she thought of his gift, Dan also felt hurt and misunderstood. These recent hard feelings were clouding their relationship. Now that they were about to take a one-week vacation together without their two children, they had fears about how this supposedly romantic getaway would go. They decided to try a structured moneytalk about the vacation and their disparate money styles.

Dan and Sondra Prepare for the Moneytalk

To clear the air somewhat before beginning their talk, Dan and Sondra decided to do a couple of exercises you're already familiar with: "Love Letters" and "My Perfect Conversation."

WRITING "LOVE LETTERS"

Dan and Sondra agreed to devote a half hour to writing "love letters" to each other in private. The subject of the letters was to be the bad feelings after the anniversary gift incident. (For more information on this technique, refer to chapter 8.) Here's Dan's love letter to Sondra:

Dear Sondra:

I feel upset that you didn't like my anniversary gift of "My Prayer," our old song. I am frustrated that I looked for hours and hours for a sentimental and romantic gift I thought would please you, and it didn't work. I am disappointed that you didn't appreciate this gift and the love and effort that went into it. I worry that whatever I do give you, it'll never be enough, or never be the right thing.

I feel bad about hurting your feelings in my choice of a gift. That was the last thing in the world I wanted to do. I know you tend to feel unloved if gifts aren't worth a lot of money, and maybe I should have remembered that in choosing this gift. I'm sorry I didn't—for both of us.

I love the times when you give me gifts that are simple and from the heart, like the poem you wrote me for our last anniversary. I appreciate all the ways you support me in my life. I love you and want to make you happy.

     Love, Dan

After writing this letter, Dan felt less hurt and angry, and much more aware of the good things in his relationship with his wife.

Here is Sondra's love letter to Dan:

Dear Dan:

I am angry that you bought me such a chintzy little gift for our anniversary. It made me feel like I wasn't worth very much to you.

I am sad that we had hurt and tension around the giving of this gift, and that these bad feelings almost spoiled our night out to celebrate our anniversary. I wish we could have resolved our differences more lovingly.

I am afraid we are so different that neither of us will ever be able to meet each other's real needs. I don't want us to drift apart—I want us to find a way to get closer.

I am sorry I reacted so strongly to the CD you bought. When I remember that money doesn't equal love, I can appreciate the sentimental and romantic nature of your gift, and the time and effort you took to get it for me.

I know you try hard to please me in a lot of ways. I'm sorry I don't tell you more often about the ways I do appreciate you. I'm sorry I tend to be so critical and attacking when I feel hurt and rejected.

I love you and will try to do better. I will try to understand that you have a different style of gift-giving than I do, and not take it to mean that you don't care. I know you do, and I do, too.

Love, Sondra

In writing her love letter, Sondra was able to let go of a large chunk of her anger and hurt, and to begin to appreciate the effort Dan had made, in his own way, to please her.

Both Dan and Sondra thought about writing "response letters" to themselves. (Remember, with a response letter you write a reaction to the love letter you have just composed, pretending to be your partner and responding with the exact words you want to hear.) But they felt so much better after writing the love letters that they decided they could dispense with the responses. They saw no need to share their love letters with each other.

Having gotten out their feelings about their anniversary, Don and Sondra were now able to move toward their moneytalk with less emotional baggage.

PRACTICING "MY PERFECT CONVERSATION"

Dan was generally a "thinking type" in his communication style, tending to talk logically and give advice in conversation. Sondra was a "feeling type" who tended to share feelings in a fairly emotional way. Because their styles were so different, they decided that doing the "perfect conversation" exercise (see chapter 8) would also be useful preparation for their moneytalk. The topic for their conversation would be stresses at work.

Sondra, a teacher, went first. She asked that Dan respond with empathetic comments such as "That must be hard" and positive comments like "You're very good at that" while looking her in the eye.

SONDRA: The kids at school are driving me crazy lately, and my principal is absolutely no help!

DAN: It must be frustrating to work in that kind of stressful environment, with so little support from your boss. I'd hate to have to deal with kids like those!

SONDRA: It is. But at least with Freddy, my most difficult kid, I see some slow signs of progress. He didn't have even one tantrum today.

DAN: I know you're a great teacher. I'd love to see you in action with him.

After this short interchange, Sondra told him what he did *right*.

SONDRA: You looked me in the eye, and responded to me sensitively when you said, "You're a great teacher" and "I'd hate to have to deal with kids like those." I love that!

Now it was Dan's turn. He wanted Sondra mainly to listen and not to make too many suggestions about what he might do differently. But he indicated he would appreciate some degree of intellectual response to the situation. This is what he said about his work stresses as a corporate executive.

DAN: My job is driving me crazy, too. This guy who works under me is a pain. He refuses to do what I tell him to do, and I feel like he's trying to undermine me. If he keeps this up, we'll never meet our deadline this month. I'm tempted to just fire him, I'm so frustrated.

SONDRA: What a difficult situation! I know you're trying your hardest.

DAN: You can't imagine how hard I work to try to get projects finished on time. But this guy is so slow! He just keeps dragging his feet.

SONDRA: You know, I've been reading about how to resolve conflict by working toward a win-win solution for both parties. Maybe if you identify a goal you both want, you could figure out a new way to approach this difficult guy.

Sondra was normally prone to saying things like "When I'm in that situation, here's what I do..." or, "You need to be more patient with...," but this time she curtailed her tendency to preach. Dan went on to give her positive feedback only.

DAN: In general, you listened well, and I felt supported by you. You didn't preach at me or tell me what I'm doing wrong. I appreciated that. I especially liked it when you told me about ideas in the field of conflict resolution about win-win solutions. That was interesting. Thank you for really hearing me.

In this positive frame of mind, Dan and Sondra were ready to progress to the more loaded topic at hand.

AGREEING ON TOPICS TO DISCUSS

Dan wanted to discuss Sondra's tendency to overspend and lose track of their money, and his fear that she would act this way on vacation. Sondra wanted to talk about Dan's tightness and money worry, and the possibility that these traits would prevent them from enjoying their time away from the kids. They agreed to talk about both topics under the subject of "fears and hopes about our vacation."

AGREEING ON GROUND RULES

To make this potentially difficult moneytalk as safe as possible, Dan and Sondra agreed to the following ground rules:

- We will not interrupt each other.
- We'll start this moneytalk sitting back-to-back, so we can stay more closely in touch with our feelings, and we'll turn around later when either of us feels the need for more eye contact. We'll definitely talk face-to-face during the positive cool-down toward the end of the moneytalk.
- We will announce in advance the nature of our communications, and ask whether the other person is willing to listen.
- We will try to avoid long, punitive tirades, limiting each communication to about three minutes.
- We will say "I'm finished" when we each feel we have completed our communication.
- We will start with positive warm-ups.
- Next, we will share grudges, hurts, and resentments, in order to try to get rid of them quickly and efficiently.
- After one person shares a difficult or emotional message, the other will try to repeat the essence of it before responding to it with an equal emotional charge.
- Finally, we'll try to negotiate about what we both want on this vacation.
- We'll agree to end the moneytalk by sharing cool-downs—positive appreciations of each other.
- We'll try to set a time for the next moneytalk.

SONDRA: I appreciate how hard you work to support us, how you do our taxes and pay bills on time, and keep our life organized around money. I also appreciate what a good father you are to the kids.

DAN: I appreciate all you do to bring joy and pleasure into our lives—me and the kids. You are generous with all of us.

Anchored in their good feelings, Dan and Sondra were willing to take the plunge into a more dangerous zone. Still, their defenses had to be addressed early on.

SHARING OLD HURTS, RESENTMENTS, AND FEARS

SONDRA: Dan, I feel upset about something. Are you willing to listen?
DAN (feeling defensive already): No. I feel defensive and need to share my fear. Are you willing to listen?

Sondra understood that Dan needed to clear the decks in his mind, so to speak, to be able to hear her. Therefore, she responded:

SONDRA: Yes. I'm willing to listen.
DAN: I bet you're going to attack me for my stinginess, and I'm sick of hearing about that. Talk about something different for a change! I'm finished.

Having vented (and gotten that defensive response off his chest), Dan was now willing to listen to Sondra.

SONDRA: I yearn to be able to discuss spending and saving, avoiding and worrying about money in a new, nonadversarial way. I'm willing to spend time getting out some old resentments, but I want to move past them quickly, and not get stuck in the old, awful, negative places. I hope you want that too. I'm finished.
DAN: I want to verify what you just said. Are you willing to listen?
SONDRA (happy about that): Yes!

DAN: You hope we can have a friendlier discussion about our differences than the blaming fights we usually have. Did I hear you as you wished to be heard?

SONDRA: Yes, you heard me 90 percent. I'm finished.

It's impossible to overstress the importance of verifying feelings and giving percentage feedback on how well the speaker feels heard. This process helps create intimacy and positive regard for each other.

DAN: I'm worried about something. Are you willing to listen?

SONDRA: Yes.

DAN: Sondra, I'm sick of living in dread of what you're gonna spend money on next. I'm sick of doing all the worrying in this family about whether we have enough for this vacation, this new piece of furniture, this new purchase for the kids. You didn't grow up with a grandfather whose family lost everything in the Depression, so you have no idea how that feels. Living with your overspending keeps me in a constant state of anxiety. I hate it, and I want it to stop! I'm finished.

Pushing out his feelings like this was new for Dan, who usually stopped short of fully expressing himself. This response enabled him to break through to a new place, and he started to blink back tears, feeling the pain of this conflict. His vulnerability melted Sondra's defenses, and she was able to verify his feelings without responding angrily or defensively.

SONDRA: I want to verify what you said. Are you willing to listen?

DAN: Yes.

SONDRA: You feel tremendously burdened by worries over money, and my unconscious way of spending too much money all the time drives you crazy. You're tired of doing all the worrying for the whole family, and you want me to stop overspending. Did I hear you as you wished to be heard?

Dan felt moved by how well Sondra had heard his feelings.

DAN: I have feedback for you. Are you willing to listen?
SONDRA: Sure.
DAN: You got it 100 percent. I'm finished.
DAN: I have a positive feeling to share. Are you willing to listen?
SONDRA: Yes.
DAN: I can't tell you how good it makes me feel that you heard me so well, so simply and clearly. Thank you so much. I'm finished.

Dan still felt stirred up, so he went on to vent his feeling:

DAN: I have another "unequal." Are you willing to listen?
SONDRA: Yes.
DAN: I'm so exhausted from overworking, worrying, and feeling alone in my concern about whether our family will always have enough. I wish you could share this burden with me more, without getting more exhausted yourself. I'm finished.

It was time for Sondra to take some time and space for her own old feelings.

SONDRA: I'm upset about something. Are you willing to listen?
DAN: Yes.
SONDRA: I hate it that you worry and overwork so much. I wish you'd spend more time with me and the kids. If you would, I might not use all my free time to run around in stores and shop. I think a part of your worry is exaggerated and a result of your terrible fearful childhood.

Now I have an attack on myself: "Sondra, you *do* need to get more conscious of your spending and stop spending to get back at Dan for not being around. It's a lousy way to conduct your life! Grow up and start asking Dan for what you really want: more time alone with him!" And you, Dan, need to listen to my good advice about working less. If you worked less, I'd spend less, and we'd both have more love in our life together.

If you won't consider this, I probably will go on overspending and driving you nuts about this forever. It's time you took my advice in an area where I *do* have some expertise: knowing how to create quality family time! I'm finished.

Now it was Dan's turn to be generous.

DAN: I want to verify what you said. Are you willing to listen?
SONDRA: Yes.
DAN: You feel that I worry and overwork too much, partly because of my difficult, fearful childhood. You want me to consider working less and spending more quality time at home, with you and the kids, and with you alone. If I did that, you would spend less money. Did I hear you as you wished to be heard?
SONDRA: I have feedback. Wanna hear it?
DAN: Sure.
SONDRA: You heard me 98 percent. I'm finished.

MOVING ON TO THE PRESENT

Just from hearing each other's irrational frustrations and mirroring them, Sondra and Dan felt much more hopeful about addressing each other's concerns about their upcoming vacation.

SONDRA: Dan, I have a concern I want to share. Are you willing to listen?

DAN: Okay.

SONDRA: I don't want to spend every minute of this vacation having you breathe down my neck about how much money I'm spending on things for myself and gifts for the kids. I want you to lighten up about this, and trust me that I won't be totally unreasonable when it comes to buying souvenirs. I'm finished.

DAN: I have a concern. Are you willing to listen?

SONDRA: Okay.

DAN: I don't want to worry that all you're going to do on vacation is buy more things we don't need. If you would agree to set limits on yourself, and tell me what those limits are, maybe I could agree to work on letting go of my money anxiety—at least for a while. But I'm afraid that with you, especially on vacation, the sky's the limit! I'm finished.

Now each partner was willing to verify the other's upset feelings.

SONDRA: I want to verify what you said. Are you willing to listen?

DAN: Yes.

SONDRA: You're afraid that unless I agree to set a ceiling on my vacation spending, I'll go wild and spend all our money, sending you into a massive anxiety attack about our money. You want me to set reasonable spending limits and tell you what they are, so you can relax. Did I hear you as you wished to be heard?

DAN (pleased that Sondra heard him well): Yes, you did—95 percent. I'm finished.

Once you are comfortable with this process, you can experiment with letting go of the requirement to ask for permission before giving feedback. However, when you are sharing stirred-up feelings of any kind (hurt, anger, fear, etc.), it's vital to ask for permission and announce the nature of your communication beforehand.

Dan went on to verify Sondra's feelings:

DAN: You feel afraid that I'm gonna breathe down your neck about spending money on this vacation, and you want me to trust you more and lay off. You enjoy buying souvenirs for yourself and the kids of places we've been, and whether I understand that or not, you want me to accept this need of yours and trust that you won't go wild. Did I hear you as you wish to be heard?

SONDRA: I would say 90 percent—and the 10 percent was just that I wished your tone of voice was warmer. Yes, I'm finished.

Both Dan and Sondra now felt that they were ready to try to negotiate about ways to deal with spending on their vacation.

Getting Aligned About Money Makes Couples Feel Fulfilled

NEGOTIATING WITH EACH OTHER

SONDRA: Dan, I have a negotiation. Are you willing to listen?

DAN: Yes.

SONDRA: I offer to spend only $100 of your money, and up to $100 of my own money, on gifts during this vacation. I want you to refrain from saying nasty things to me about what I buy or acting grouchy in any way about my souvenir shopping. I want you to look pleasant about this, even if you are still feeling somewhat anxious. I'm finished.

DAN: I have a negotiation. Are you willing to listen?

SONDRA: Yes.

DAN: I offer to act pleasant, upbeat, and nonjudgmental about your shopping on vacation. I would like you to spend only $75 of my money, and I would prefer it if you spent only $75 of your own money, but that's up to you. I'm finished.

SONDRA: I have a little angry feeling. Are you willing to listen?

DAN: Okay.

SONDRA: I feel like a bad kid when you try to tell me how much to spend. I hate it! I also have an attack on myself: "Sondra, if you would set real limits on yourself, your husband wouldn't have to set them for you! Grow up!" I'm finished.

Now that Sondra had expressed these sentiments, she could return to negotiation:

SONDRA: Dan, I have a negotiation. Are you willing to listen?

DAN: Yes.

SONDRA: I accept your negotiation. I'm finished.

Dan and Sondra felt quite pleased with how well their moneytalk had gone. They had made some real progress: in communicating more equally, in understanding each other better, and in taking some positive action.

CONCLUDING WITH THE COOL-DOWN: MORE APPRECIATIONS

DAN: I appreciated how well you heard me, and that you were willing to set a concrete limit on your own spending. I know that's hard for you to do, and I want to tell you how much it means to me that you are willing to do it. I will also think about working fewer hours to spend more time with you and the kids. I really would like that too.

SONDRA: I also appreciated your willingness to hear me so sensitively. Your openness made me feel safer with you and closer to you than I've felt in ages. And I was moved by your vulnerability in sharing your pain about money worry with me. I will try to be more conscious of my spending and talk with you about it more often.

SETTING A TIME FOR THE NEXT MONEYTALK

Dan and Sondra agreed to sit down again one week after their vacation ended to see how it turned out in terms of spending and communication about money. Both of them felt very good about their new way of talking about the thorny issues in their shared moneylife.

Having Your Own Structured Moneytalk

When conducting your own structured moneytalk on a loaded topic, remember these key points:

Choose an unstressful time. Try to select a time for your moneytalk when you are not under a great deal of stress—i.e., not when the children are around, when it's tax time, or when you have to make a big money decision. If you have no choice, remember that fatigue or stress will probably make you revert to old, somewhat dysfunctional behaviors. Structured communication will help limit these bad effects, but it's not a magic formula, just a set of helpful guidelines. The best way to prepare for a moneytalk is to be in a relaxed and rested frame of mind.

Choose your topic in advance. If you haven't already identified an issue to discuss, turn back to chapter 7 and select one or two areas of polarization or chronic conflict over money that you would both like to resolve. As you decide on your topic, pay close attention to the feelings that surface; you will need to share them early on in your moneytalk. If you each choose different topics, draw lots to see which one gets discussed first. Using the suggested techniques, you should be able to handle them both in the same structured conversation.

If you feel hurt, try a "love letter." If you are holding on to any past hurts or angers connected to your chosen topic, consider writing love letters to each other about it, along with the ideal response you would like to receive. Then, unless either of you has a pressing need to share the contents of your love letter, simply move on to the next stage of the moneytalk.

Frustrated? A "perfect conversation" may help. If you tend to get frustrated communicating with your partner and feel you are not heard often enough, practice the "my perfect conversation" exercise. It will teach your partner what you need and want in conversations. You will also learn your partner's preferences in this regard.

Agree on certain ground rules. Consider adopting the ones Dan and Sondra used earlier in this chapter. Or return to the guidelines listed in chapter 8 and decide which ones would work best for your relationship.

Settle on a format for your talk. Generally speaking, this sequence works well:

- Warming up with positive strokes
- Sharing old grudges, hurts, and resentments
- Verifying your partner's feelings before going on to your own emotional reactions
- Negotiating for change
- Sharing positive cool-downs in which you validate your partner's efforts and your own as well

Decide when to meet for the next moneytalk (if possible).

Reward yourself for positive behavior. If you agree to take new actions, reward yourselves for your changes. Monitor and write down your reactions to them.

As we said earlier, you may hesitate to attempt a conversation with this highly structured process. But give it a try! If you find you prefer a simpler format, Harville Hendrix's mirroring exercise is an alternative way to create safety and deepen intimacy. You might try them both and see which one works better for you.

In many cases, our usual ways of discussing emotional subjects lead to misunderstandings, win-lose arguments, and sometimes an explosion of blame and hurt feelings. The techniques of a structured moneytalk create safe boundaries within which to confront difficult feelings, and a process with which to resolve them.

11.
GOAL SETTING: ACHIEVING MUTUALITY AND MONEY HARMONY

Now you are ready for the final step in your journey toward money harmony: learning the skills involved in productive goal setting, first alone and then with your partner.

If the mere suggestion of mutual goal-setting makes you feel nervous and stirred up ("We want two different things; I'm sure we'll never be able to work it out!"), hearken to some words of encouragement. Experts in the field of conflict resolution tell us that although people's goals may be different, they're not usually in direct opposition.[23] If both partners take the time to communicate what they really need and want, they are often able to create solutions that work well for each of them. Goals that at first seem to conflict may not be mutually exclusive after all.

So have faith! If you work to clarify your most important life goals, later in this chapter you will find the help you need to harmonize your goals with your partner's.

Setting Goals for Yourself

Before attempting to discuss individual and shared goals with your mate, you need to learn about your own style of goal-setting. Are you able to envision what you might want to do or be in the future? Do you plan, or just dream? Do you tend to focus on the near future, a few years down the road, or many years distant? Or do you resist thinking about goals at all?

If you do have goals, you need to determine which ones persist over time and which seem more fleeting; which ones involve you alone and which involve your partner and/or your family; which ones would require you to come up with more money; and finally, what steps—financial or otherwise—you would need to take to reach them.

FANTASIZE ABOUT WHAT YOU WANT

Is it easy for you to envision what you want in life and figure out how to attain it? Some people love to do this. Others fantasize so much that it prevents them from moving ahead in reality. Still others are afraid to imagine what they want. They live with a kind of superstitious pessimism: "If I let myself want something too much, I'll be devastated if I don't get it. It's better not to think about it at all." If this describes you, you need to challenge your fear and open up to the possibility of imagining what you truly want and need. Unless you can visualize it or imagine it in some other way, you'll find it very difficult to achieve.

So when you are relaxed and at ease, take some time to let yourself conjure up pictures, feelings, and sounds of what you would like to achieve or attain for yourself in the future. Do you want to take a trip to Paris with your partner? Would you like to begin taking piano lessons? Do you have a desire to go to graduate school? Do you want to train for a new profession? Or maybe just learn better computer skills? Whatever it is, give yourself permission to want it, first and foremost, with all your heart. That will pave the way for your being able to have it.

To organize your thoughts, write down your goals for each of these time periods:
- Short term (up to a year from now)
- Medium term (one to five years away)
- Long term (more than five years away)

If you prefer to define these periods differently, that's fine. Just try to set timelines that you and your partner can agree on.

Was it difficult for you to identify your goals? If so, try the following exercise.

WRITE YOUR OWN IMAGINARY BIOGRAPHY

Imagine, in as much detail as possible, how your biography will appear in Wikipedia when you are gone. Write it all out, including everything you want to have achieved during your lifetime. This assignment is astonishing in its power to clarify the kind of life you'd most want to have.

NOTICE YOUR NATURAL TENDENCIES AROUND GOAL-SETTING

Do you think about goals mainly in the very short term? For example, maybe you muse about a romantic bed-and-breakfast vacation with your mate... or about buying something for your kids... or achieving something specific in your work… goals that are all in the next month or two.

Or are you thinking little bit farther into the future? Do you want to send your children to sleep-away camp in six months? Are you planning to save your next bonus for the kids' college fund? Would you like to replace your old car sometime later this year?

Perhaps your goals are much longer term. Do you plan to change professions or get more professional training in three to five years? Would you like to move in the next seven to 10 years, when the kids are out of college? Do you think about retiring 10 or 15 years from now?

Try to identify a few goals that cover time intervals you tend to ignore. If you're a short-term goal setter, for example, generate a couple of long-term goals. Also, spend some time thinking about types of goals that you tend to overlook. If you always focus on career goals, come up with a few goals involving hobbies or vacations. Notice whether you think about your goals in vague terms or plan them out in nitty-gritty detail. Whichever tendency you exhibit, try the opposite to give yourself more flexibility.

As you review your goal list, indicate for each goal...

- How soon you would like to achieve it
- Whether it will cost money to achieve it
- If so, how much money you will need and
- How you might get the necessary money to achieve the goal

YOUR GOAL LIST: ONCE IS NOT ENOUGH

Make a list of your goals *at least three times*. You can create this list once a week, every other week, or once a month. When you work on a new list, avoid looking at previous ones. The important thing is to notice afterward which goals come up time and time again.

Again, specify when you want to attain these goals, whether it will cost money to attain them, how much money you will need, and where the money might come from.

GOAL SETTING

If you give yourself the time and space to generate a list of goals at least three times, you will have identified more trustworthy, abiding goals as opposed to impulsive fantasies that may change from week to week, or month to month.

ARE YOU SABOTAGING YOUR GOALS?

Do you tend to procrastinate? Do you feel anxious if things go too well? Are you afraid of having more pleasure in your life, or more educational status, or more wealth, than your parents had (or have)? If so, you might write out an imaginary conversation with one or both parents in which they give you permission to surpass them in some way. See if this exercise helps reverse the patterns that may be holding you back from reaching some of your goals.

Many of us fear the possibility of new pleasure more than our old familiar pain. Why? Because pleasure threatens to sweep us away into areas we haven't experienced before, whereas old pain is as familiar and comfortable as an old shoe. We all need to work toward being able to "tolerate" new pleasure by letting go of our old pain, even though we identify with it so strongly.

ONE MORE LOOK AT YOUR GOALS
BEFORE MEETING WITH YOUR PARTNER

As a final exercise, look over the list of goals that surfaced again and again, and prioritize them in this way:

- Put a *1* after the goals that are most important to you, the ones you would be terribly disappointed not to meet.
- Put a *2* after the goals you want a lot but could live without, if necessary.
- Put a *3* after the goals you could give up most easily if you had to.

This is not to say that you can't achieve most or all of your goals. It's just a clarification of which ones are truly at the top of your list.

Make sure you have thought about the implications for your moneylife of every goal you include. Will it cost money? How much? And how will you go about earning, saving, finding that money in your budget? If you are a Dreamer and not a Planner, this part may be hard for you. But it's worthwhile to practice the nonhabitual by getting specific if you tend to be vague. This will lead you closer to your goals.

Meeting in the Middle

GOAL SETTING

Sharing Your Goals with Your Partner

After you and your partner have each developed a list of tried-and-true goals (some of them personal and others involving you both), it's time to meet and share the results.

You may want to sit back-to-back and communicate this information in the structured moneytalk format, announcing your intent to share and asking whether your partner is willing to listen. Or you may feel comfortable enough to talk face-to-face without any structure, using the mirroring exercise.

If either of you panics upon hearing about goals you don't share, go into the structured or mirroring format, share your fears (if the other is willing to listen, of course), and try to verify or mirror what each of you wants and how your partner is feeling about these goals.

It's crucial to remember that even if you and your partner have different goals, you will almost always be able to succeed as long as you are both committed to finding a way you both can satisfy your deepest needs and yearnings. Don't be afraid to slow down the process; it may take time to find a solution that works for you both. Remember Mark and Kate, the Planner-Dreamer couple? When they started therapy, Mark wanted to teach emotionally disturbed kids for very low pay. Kate, who was still finishing her graduate degree, worried about how to put their daughter through college if he pursued his dream. By tuning in to the dreams of the Planner, Kate, who longed to live abroad, while the Dreamer, Mark, planned in detail how to accomplish a career change, they found a dream and a plan they both could share: living abroad for a few years. During this time, Kate finished her graduate degree and Mark tried out the field he was considering, without interrupting their daughter's education.

The final step is to merge your list of goals with your partner's. You'll end up with a set of joint goals and two sets of individual goals. The final goals on these lists should be such that both of you get most of what you truly desire. Remember to keep in mind how much it would cost to realize these dreams, and brainstorm about how you might achieve them. If it looks unlikely that you will be able to accomplish a particular goal, discuss alternative ways to satisfy at least some of your yearnings.

Downsizing Your Goals in Times of Stress

It's extremely difficult to have to downsize your goals or put them off because of financial hardship or another unexpected development. A serious injury or illness, a job loss, or the need to provide care for an elderly parent can wreak havoc on your plans. This procedure may help you handle the stress:

- Sit back-to-back and use the structured communication format, or sit face-to-face and do the mirroring exercise.
- Share your feelings of loss, pain, disappointment, or even panic about having to put off certain goals.
- Mirror or verify each other's feelings about this sad turn of events.
- Figure out ways you can nourish yourselves during this period, both individually and together, that cost little or no money. (When people are asked what activities make them happy, many things on their list are usually free or inexpensive.)
- Discuss how you can eventually achieve these goals; or modify them to make them more attainable.

If adversity derails your progress toward your goals, remind yourself, "This, too, shall pass." Recognizing that your period of sacrifice is finite, and that other sources of nourishment and pleasure may substitute for the ones you can't afford now, will help you overcome panic and move on to positive attitudes and actions.

Your Last "Money Harmony" Exercise

We hope that after undertaking the process in *Money Harmony*, you and your partner feel safe enough with each other to do the following—and final—exercise.

Spend a little time with your partner meditating on the state of money harmony. That is, consider how things would be if you felt totally at ease with money, as an individual and in your life as a couple. Close your eyes, breathe deeply, and come up with some mental images and sensations of this state of satisfaction and peace.

Then, ask yourselves what steps you could take right now to move toward this state. See if you are willing to commit to taking at least one of those steps, either alone or together. If you do, reward yourself for taking this action and monitor the way you feel after having taken it.

A Family Enjoying Money Harmony

Your Progress Toward Money Harmony

Congratulations on doing all the hard work involved in increasing your self-awareness and changing your behavior around money. You now understand that money is not Love, Power, Happiness, Self-Worth, or Security—not even security in old age. It's only a tool to accomplish some of your life's goals.

If you have a partner, you now have the awareness and the techniques to communicate respectfully and creatively about the differences in your relationship with money. You have learned to validate your partner's strengths as well as your own, to move toward the middle, and to practice walking in each other's moccasins.

No longer will money be an obstacle or a source of tension in your life. From now on you can use it to enhance your sense of ful-fillment and intimacy as you continue making progress toward money harmony.

We wish you well on your journey.

NOTES

1. These "Readers on Wealth" letters appeared in the April 1989 issue of *The Sun*. It was startling to see how many of the letters disputed the connection between financial wealth and real wealth (a feeling of abundance that comes from deep fulfillment).

2. Warren Farrell expresses this thought in *Why Men Are the Way They Are: The Male-Female Dynamic*. Farrell has spent many years exploring numerous aspects of power and powerlessness in our culture. He has tried to help both men and women deal with their own powerlessness without blaming each other for their situation, so that the two sexes can achieve real control over their own lives instead of power over each other.

3. David Keirsey and Marilyn Bates, *Please Understand Me: Character and Temperament Types*. This statistic is found in many books by Myers-Briggs practitioners. Some authors say that the statistic is closer to two-thirds; that is, two-thirds of men are thinking types, and two-thirds of women are feeling types.

4. This comparison of decision-making styles is found in *Type Talk: The 16 Personality Types That Determine How We Live, Love, and Work,* by Otto Kroeger and Janet M. Thuesen.

5. Deborah Tannen discusses these and many related differences between the sexes in chapter 6 of *You Just Don't Understand.*

6. Liz Davidson of Financial Finesse, "How Advisors Can End the Real 'War Against Women,'" ThinkAdvisor.com, June 28, 2012.

7. For a discussion of how these differences are manifested, see *You Just Don't Understand.*

8. John Gray, *Men Are from Mars, Women Are from Venus.*

9. James J. Green, "Women Are an Opportunity, Not a Niche: Schwab's Clark," ThinkAdvisor.com, July 2, 2012.

10. Lauren Weber & Sue Shellenbarger, "Office Stress: His vs. Hers," *The Wall Street Journal,* updated March 4, 2013.

11. Donald Katz speculates that women may be "less comfortable using money as an agent of control" in "Men, Women, and Money: The Last Taboo," *Worth,* June 1993.

12. Katz also says that "divorced husbands' standards of living tend to rise by 40%, whereas divorced women's incomes fall by an average of 70%."

13. "Women and Financial Independence," Schwab Advisory Services, 2012, reported by James J. Green, "Surprise! HNW Women Want

Investment Performance From Their Advisors," ThinkAdvisor.com, June 29, 2012.

14. Susan Weidman Schneider, "Jewish Women's Philanthropy: What Do We Need to Know?" *Lilith,* Winter 1993.

15. Weber & Shellenbarger, op. cit.

16. "Controlling the Fires of Marital Conflict: Constructive and Destructive Strategies to Manage Anger," by Clifford I. Notarius and Howard J. Markman, presented at the Maryland Psychological Association/Foundation 1990–91 Postdoctoral Institute Workshop, December 7, 1990, in Columbia, Maryland.

17. Victoria Felton-Collins uses these terms in her book *Couples and Money: Why Money Interferes with Love and What to Do About It,* which she wrote with Suzanne Blair Brown.

18. Note from Olivia: In developing my couples communication techniques, I have been influenced by several experts. Isaiah Zimmerman, a clinical psychologist in Washington, D.C., created a structured communication technique he called the "Format," which I have used and adapted in my couples therapy. In his excellent article for the Washington Ethical Society, "Why Love Fails," Don Montagna, head of the society, outlines the power-struggle phase of relationships and paves the way for what he calls "no-fault love." His conceptual view parallels my own quite closely. Thomas Gordon's book, *P.E.T. Parent Effectiveness Training,* stresses the importance of using "I-messages" to minimize blame and "dumping" in communications. Lillian Rubin, Deborah Tannen, John Gray, and Warren Farrell have many interesting and important things to say about male-female differences.

Finally, John Gray and Harville Hendrix have developed some valuable couples therapy techniques. Hendrix's way of looking at couple relationships is very close to my own: namely, that the two members of a couple can help heal each other's early psychological wounds over time, while doing the work necessary to heal themselves individually.

19. In *Getting to Yes: Negotiating Agreement Without Giving In,* Roger Fisher and William Ury give two famous examples of win-win solutions. In the first, two daughters are fighting over an orange. The mother, tired and rushed, cuts the orange in half and gives each daughter one half. Both are unsatisfied. Why? Because one wanted the skin of the orange to make an orange cake, and the other wanted to eat the pulp. If the mother had taken the time and energy to ask each daughter what she wanted the orange for, she could have given each one exactly what they wanted.

The second example describes a situation in a library. One man asks the librarian if he can open the window near him, because it's hot and stuffy. The other man, seated near him, complains of a draft. The librarian, in true win-win style, closes that window, and opens another one far away, which gives the first man the breeze he wants and avoids annoying his neighbor. Both examples show us that when we probe deeply enough into each other's needs, wants, and motivations, new solutions arise that can often satisfy two parties' seemingly divergent needs.

20. Note from Olivia: Over the years, I have heard Warren Farrell talk on this subject in many presentations about male-female differences. He also writes about it in his book *Why Men Are the Way They Are: The Male-Female Dynamic.*

21. Note from Olivia: I learned this version of the exercise directly from Hendrix, at a workshop he gave on couples communication at the

NOTES

Common Boundary Conference in Washington, D.C., in November 1992. Other excellent exercises, including a different version of a mirroring exercise, are found in his book *Getting the Love You Want: A Guide for Couples*.

22. John Gray's love letter technique appears in several of his books, including *Men Are from Mars, Women Are from Venus*.

23. Fisher and Ury's book is one of the first and best primers for teaching win-win solutions.

FURTHER RESOURCES

Psychology of Money

The Secret Language of Money (audio CD set), Olivia Mellan. (CD 1: Take Charge of Your Money: Mastering Your Money Style; CD 2: Men, Women and Money: Overcoming Money Conflicts)

Crazy About Money: How Emotions Confuse Our Money Choices and What To Do About It, Maggie Baker, Ph.D. (2010)

The Financial Wisdom of Ebenezer Scrooge: 5 Principles to Transform Your Relationship with Money, Ted Klontz, Ph.D, Rick Kahler, MS, CFP®, & Brad Klontz, Psy.D. (2010)

Mind Over Money: Overcoming the Money Disorders That Threaten Our Financial Health, Brad Klontz, Psy.D, & Ted Klontz, Ph.D. (2009)

Financial Advisors

Certified Financial Planners: http://letsmakeaplan.org

National Association of Personal Financial Planners (NAPFA): www.napfa.org

The Garrett Network: www.GarrettPlanningNetwork.com

Financial Fitness and Budgeting

The Budget Kit:The Common Cents Money Management Workbook (sixth edition), Judy Lawrence. (2011)
Creating Wealth From The Inside Out Workbook, Kathleen Burns Kingsbury. (2010)
7 Money Rules for Life®: How to Take Control of Your Financial Future, Mary Hunt. (2012)

Gender Differences

The Female Brain, Louann Brizendine, MD. (2007)
Intimate Strangers: Men and Women Together, Lillian B. Rubin. (1984) (Though published a while ago, this book still has true differences to share.)
The Male Brain, Louann Brizendine, MD. (2010)
You Just Don't Understand: Women and Men in Conversation, Deborah Tannen. (2007)

Kids and Money

Raising Financially Confident Kids, Mary Hunt. (2012)
Raising Money Smart Kids: What They Need to Know About Money and How to Tell Them (Kiplinger's Personal Finance), Janet Bodnar. (2005)

Men and Money

Why Men Earn More: The Startling Truth Behind the Pay Gap – and What Women Can Do About It, Warren Farrell, Ph.D. (2004)

Money, Meaning and Spirituality

Blessing the Hands That Feed Us, Vicki Robin. (2014)
The Energy of Money: A Spiritual Guide to Financial and Personal Fulfillment, Maria Nemeth, Ph.D. (2000)
The Soul of Money: Reclaiming the Wealth of Our Inner Resources, Lynne Twist. (2006)
Your Money or Your Life: 9 Steps to Transforming Your Relationship with Money and Achieving Financial Independence: Revised and Updated for the 21st Century, Vicki Robin, Joe Dominguez & Monique Tilford. (2008)

Overspending

Overcoming Overspending: A Winning Plan for Spenders and Their Partners, Olivia Mellan & Sherry Christie. (2009)
Bought Out and $pent!: Recovering from Compulsive Shopping and Spending, Terrance Daryl Shulman, JD, LMSW. (2008)
Cluttered Lives, Empty Souls: Compulsive Stealing, Spending & Hoarding, Terrance Daryl Shulman, JD, LMSW. (2011)
To Buy or Not to Buy: Why We Overshop and How to Stop, April Lane Benson, Ph.D. (2008)

Retirement and The Third Age (not just about money)

Couple's Retirement Puzzle: 10 Must-Have Conversations for Transitioning to the Second Half of Life, Roberta K. Taylor, M. Ed., & Dorian Mintzer, Ph.D. (2012)
Project Renewment: The First Retirement Model for Career Women, Bernice Bratter & Helen Dennis. (2008)

The Third Age: Six Principles for Personal Growth and Rejuvenation After Forty, William A. Sadler, Ph.D. (2001)

Support Groups

Debtors Anonymous: www.debtorsanonymous.org
Gamblers Anonymous: www.gamblersanonymous.org

Underearning (for Women)

Overcoming Underearning: A Five Step Plan to a Richer Life, Barbara Stanny. (2007)
Secrets of Six-Figure Women: Surprising Strategies to Up Your Earnings and Change Your Life, Barbara Stanny. (2004)
Why Women Earn Less: How to Make What You're Really Worth, Mikelann R. Valterra. (2004)

Wealthy Families

Beating the Midas Curse, Perry L. Cochell & Rodney C. Zeeb. (2005)

Women and Money

Money Shy to Money Sure: A Woman's Road Map to Financial Well-Being, Olivia Mellan & Sherry Christie. (2001)
Kiplinger's Money Smart Women: Everything You Need to Know to Achieve a Lifetime of Financial Security (Kiplinger's Personal Finance), Janet Bodnar. (2006)
Prince Charming Isn't Coming: How Women Get Smart About Money, Barbara Stanny. (2007)

Resources for Therapists, Coaches, and Financial Advisors

The Client Connection: How Advisors Can Build Bridges That Last, Olivia Mellan & Sherry Christie. (2009)

The Advisors' Guide to Money Psychology, Olivia Mellan & Sherry Christie. (2002)

How to Give Financial Advice to Couples: Essential Skills for Balancing High-Net-Worth Clients' Needs, Kathleen Burns Kingsbury. (2013)

How to Give Financial Advice to Women: Attracting & Retaining High-Net-Worth Female Clients, Kathleen Burns Kingsbury. (2012)

OLIVIA'S ACKNOWLEDGMENTS

I feel grateful to many friends and colleagues who have made writing this book so pleasurable and satisfying for me.

First, to Michael Goldberg, who created Money Harmony work with me in the early 1980s, who developed the first money personality types, and who helped train therapists in California with me. We presented our work together that first year.

Thanks to Barbara Monteiro, who brought my first self-published workbook to Walker and Company (now Bloomsbury), where George Gibson helped me transform it into this, my first book. George was a delight and inspiration; he has been a true friend and source of support in all ways. Jackie Johnson helped us clarify our vision. I appreciate this wonderful firm's integrity and willingness to involve Sherry and me in all aspects of the publication process, and their help in transferring publication rights back to me in this revised and updated edition.

To all the clients, whether in my therapy or coaching practice, who have deepened my appreciation of the complexity of the journey around money dysfunction and related issues, and who have pushed me forward in my own internal process as well: thanks for being willing to share your journey with others so that they might learn enough to begin healing and make new, more fulfilling choices around money and life goals.

My gratitude to other money therapists, workshop leaders, and consultants in the field of money psychology and money coaching: Maggie Baker, April Benson, Lynne Hornyak, Dorian Mintzer, Barbara Mitchell, Karen McCall, Barbara Stanny, Ted Klontz, and more recently, Judith Gruber and Judith Barr. Thanks to the people I "met" in my teleclasses and on my radio show in Philadelphia: Bari Tessler, Leslie Cunningham, Louisa Foster, Laura Longville, and Mikelann Valterra, among others. And many thanks to Vicki Robin and the late Joe Dominguez for their powerful work to transform our overconsumption and our way of being with money.

I also owe a great deal to my financial advisor friends and those in the planning field: Peg Downey, Dick Vodra, Mary Malgoire, Jennifer Lazarus, Marie DeCaprio, Barbara Shapiro, Eileen Michaels, Dave Drucker, Candi Kaplan, Sheryl Garrett, Susan Bradley, Cissy Elinoff, Elizabeth Jetton, Eleanor Blayney, Lauren Locker, Karen Ramsay, and Rick Kahler, therapeutic educators in the best sense of the word; and to Jamie Green, Sherry's and my perfect editor at *Investment Advisor* magazine (www.thinkadvisor.com), for all his support and his warm friendship. To all the money professionals who have believed in me and felt I had something unique to offer to their field, thank you for your confidence and your enthusiasm.

Deep appreciation to my close personal friends, Nancy Dunn (my son's "fairy godmother"), to the members of my couples' group for the last 20-plus years, to April Moore and Andy Schmookler, and to my brother Stu and his wife, Nancy, and family, for giving me the personal support necessary to persevere with a process that I find so challenging. Thanks to Susan (Sandi) England for her business acumen, her friendship, and her generosity. I also owe a sincere thank-you to Anne Anderson, who made my first Money Personality quiz and first workbook possible; to my dear friends at the Washington Therapy Guild (Ruthie, Steph, Anne again, Rachel, Joe, and Don), my original professional work "family," and to Louise Klok, who helps me do the deepest work on myself so I can try to "walk my talk."

In my own moneylife, I most cherish the financial wisdom of my husband, Michael, who is a model of sanity, balance, and nonjudgmental good advice. Love and appreciation to my son Anil, whose honesty in discussions and natural frugality always teach me something, to my sons Bennett and Scott, and to my grandkids—Asia Camille, DJ, Eva Olivia (!), and Bodhin Tadeo—and their mothers, Carlissa, Courage, and Heather, for who they are and for making my family life such a joy.

And finally, my deepest thanks to Sherry Christie, my brilliant writing and editing partner since 1995, for a perfect working partnership, and for her ability to tune in to the intent of my words and translate my message so much better than I could ever have done on my own.

SHERRY'S ACKNOWLEDGMENTS

On that May afternoon in 1993, little did I know that the woman I was interviewing for a client newsletter would become my friend and work partner for the next 20-plus years. Not only have I learned a great deal from Olivia Mellan about why people think and feel the way they do about their finances, but I've reveled in voicing the wisdom of this inspired, dynamic, and articulate Muse of money psychology. Respecting each other's strengths, we have successfully collaborated on five books so far, as well as hundreds of articles for *Investment Advisor* and its sister media. Olivia's warm friendship and encouragement have transformed the two of us, former college classmates, into colleagues in a partnership made in heaven.

I'd also like to acknowledge my debt to several other wonderful people. Although some have passed on, I expect they are still thinking up jokes to play on each other in heaven.

First, to John Schacht, teacher of honors math at Bexley High, who treated me as one of the guys (some of whom went on to become aerospace engineers, investment industry leaders, and other kinds of brainiacs). From Mr. Schacht I learned to love math, a language every woman ought to speak fluently.

To Mary Cantwell, head of the editorial copywriting department at *Mademoiselle,* who showed me it was possible to be paid for having fun with words.

To Bill Kight, Ron Cowman, Dewey Abram, and Jack Haunty, a quartet of Mad Men from whom a flaky writer learned to become a disciplined marketer; a starry-eyed idealist, to believe in free enterprise; and a young woman, to become a leader of men. Bill, Ron, Dewey, and Jack made me a vice president before I was 30, and hired me back twice when I strayed. Everyone should have the opportunity to work in an equal-opportunity talent garden like theirs.

To John Fisher and John Russell, marketing chiefs at tiny City National Bank in Columbus, later Bank One, later JPMorgan Chase. Fisher and Russell turned conventional banking on its ear with offbeat ideas like Honor Bonds payable to bearer (the IRS would only know if you told them), as well as BankAmericards and ATMs, which CNB was among the first in the nation to introduce. From them I learned that when it comes to pleasing customers, smarts are more important than size.

To Julie English, who jump-started my freelance financial writing business (now in its 22nd year) with a complicated project that kept me going for months. Thank you, Julie, for believing in me.

To the many other clients over the years who have helped me explore the ins and outs of financial services: You're the nicest people I've ever met, and I'm immensely grateful that you chose to work with me. Special thanks to the 99.9% of you who paid me on time.

Finally, my deepest appreciation goes to F. Leon Herron, the retired CEO of O.M. Scott & Sons (now Scotts MiracleGro). Le Herron has been a mentor to me for nearly 40 years—part role model, part coach, part father figure, and part guide to the responsibilities of leadership. Working with him on the company memos that became

Sharing Some Thoughts and *One Man's Opinion* was both a pleasure and an education. More recently, our collaboration on *Making Your Company Human: Inspiring Others to Reach Their Potential* has been pure joy.

Le has always maintained that leading people isn't about what you get out of it, but what they get out of it. He may be a little ahead of his time. But that time, I feel sure, is coming.

INDEX

INDEX

INDEX

CPSIA information can be obtained
at www.ICGtesting.com
Printed in the USA
LVHW02s1818150518
577262LV00014B/1038/P